Linda Barrett Osborne

COME ON IN, AMERICA

AMERICA

The United States in World War I

Abrams Books for Young Readers
New York

308/4 4920

R

**For Bob, who relived World War I with me
day after day and never lost interest**

Library of Congress Cataloging-in-Publication Data
Names: Osborne, Linda Barrett, 1949– author.
Title: Come on in, America : the United States and World War I /
Linda Barrett Osborne.
Description: New York : Abrams Books for Young Readers, 2017. |
Includes bibliographical references and index.
Identifiers: LCCN 2016036830 | ISBN 9781419723780
Subjects: LCSH: World War, 1914–1918—United States—Juvenile literature. |
World War, 1914–1918—Juvenile literature.
Classification: LCC D522.7 .O73 2017 | DDC 940.3/73—dc23
LC record available at https://lccn.loc.gov/2016036830

Text copyright © 2017 Linda Barrett Osborne
Book design by Pamela Notarantonio
For image credits, see page 166.

Printed and bound in U.S.A.
10 9 8 7 6 5 4 3 2 1

ABRAMS The Art of Books
115 West 18th Street, New York, NY 10011
abramsbooks.com

Contents

Introduction   1

Chapter 1 War Begins in Europe   7

Chapter 2 The United States Stays Neutral—or Does It? 21

Chapter 3 The United States Joins the Fight 37

Chapter 4 New and Improved Weapons 55

Chapter 5 The War on Our Home Front 71

Chapter 6 African Americans at War and at Home 97

Chapter 7 Women, Suffrage, and Service 113

Chapter 8 Peace with Victory and a Price 127

Chapter 9 War's Legacy 137

Time Line of Key Events 147

Notes 155

Selected Bibliography 164

Image Credits 166

Acknowledgments 167

Index 168

He is keeping the World safe for Democracy
Enlist and help him
C Carleton

Introduction

On April 6, 1917, the United States Congress, following President Woodrow Wilson's request, declared war on Germany. Germany, the Austro-Hungarian Empire, and the other "Central Powers" had been at war with Britain, France, Russia, and the other "Allied Countries" since 1914. The U.S. government, led by Wilson, had tried to remain neutral, not taking sides. At first, most Americans agreed the country should stay out of the messy, deadly European conflict. But as the war continued, staying neutral became more complicated. Large immigrant populations in the United States, including those from the warring countries, supported different sides in Europe. Lending money and selling weapons and other products to nations at war was good for American businesses. Some Americans, if not eager for battle, wanted to train an army to be prepared in case of war. Others were pacifists who believed war was morally wrong. Both those who believed in "preparedness" and those who believed in pacifism expressed strong views in Congress, in newspapers and magazines, and in public speeches.

This poster plays on a phrase made famous by President Woodrow Wilson—
"The world must be made safe for democracy"—in calling men to join the navy
after the United States entered World War I.

I

In early 1917, Germany's renewed policy of torpedoing merchant and passenger ships—even American ships—on their way to Allied Countries was the apparent cause that led to the American declaration of war. But the underlying reasons were more complex. They included the desire of American businesses to continue trading for profit and Wilson's own mission: to be one of the Allies and thus better able to influence the terms of peace. When he asked Congress to declare war, Wilson spoke about the attacks at sea—"we will not choose the path of submission and suffer the most sacred rights of our nation and our people to be ignored or violated." He spoke against the German government, which he called "autocratic"—ruled only and absolutely by Kaiser [Emperor] Wilhelm II and not by elected officials: ". . . the menace to . . . peace and freedom lies in the existence of autocratic governments backed by organized force which is controlled wholly by their will, not by the will of their people."

"The world must be made safe for democracy," Wilson famously stated. "Its peace must be planted upon the tested foundations of political liberty. We have no selfish ends to serve. . . . We shall be satisfied when those rights have been made as secure as the faith and the freedom of nations can make them." He concluded, "the right is more precious than peace, and we shall fight for the things which we have always carried nearest our hearts—for democracy, for the right of those who submit to authority to have a voice in their own governments, . . . for a universal dominion of right by such a concert of free peoples as shall bring peace and safety to all nations and make the world itself at last free."

With such idealistic aspirations on record, the United States entered World War I. It was in the war for nineteen months. Although many believed the fighting would last longer, the warring countries declared a truce on November 11, 1918. In all, an estimated 9 to 10 million soldiers died. The

The *Sontay* was a French ship that was torpedoed by a German submarine in the Mediterranean Sea on April 16, 1918. Rescue boats lowered from the ship saved 299 of the 344 passengers aboard. The German policy of attacking passenger and merchant ships was one of the reasons the United States went to war.

United States sent about 2 million men and women to Europe; approximately 53,500 Americans were killed in battle, and 63,000 more died from disease and accidents. Because we fought for a relatively short time and lost fewer people killed or wounded—compared with other countries—World War I has not been at the forefront of America's memory. We pay much more attention to World War II, the Vietnam War, and conflicts of the twenty-first century, and also, looking back, to the American Revolutionary War and the Civil War.

Yet in addition to the military experience in Europe, and the grief for those who died overseas, the United States experienced momentous changes at home brought on by what was at first called "the Great War," then "the World War," and then (following World War II) "World War I." The conflict marked the beginning of total modern warfare on a scale never before seen. The federal government became involved in business and personal affairs at a new level. The United States became the world's economic leader. The war changed the boundaries of disloyalty and censorship. Americans were told they were fighting a war for democracy, but with racial segregation rampant in the United States, new laws passed against dissent and espionage, and bankers and industrial leaders gaining increased influence and power, what did democracy mean?

Today, with war and terrorist threats worldwide, we again face the same questions that Americans faced during World War I. How do we protect ourselves as a country? How do we portray the "enemy"? (Woodrow Wilson made a distinction between the German government and the German people, although many Americans did not.) How do we fight stereotypes and prejudice? How do we preserve civil and political rights while also maintaining security? Should rights be sacrificed for safety? How do we live with and confront fear?

World War I provides a context for understanding the politics, policies, and attitudes of the United States today. A hundred years after the "war to end all wars," we are still looking for answers.

A phosphorous bomb—made with a chemical that lights up the sky—goes off in Gondrecourt, France. New and "improved" weapons in World War I killed millions of soldiers in battle, including 53,500 Americans.

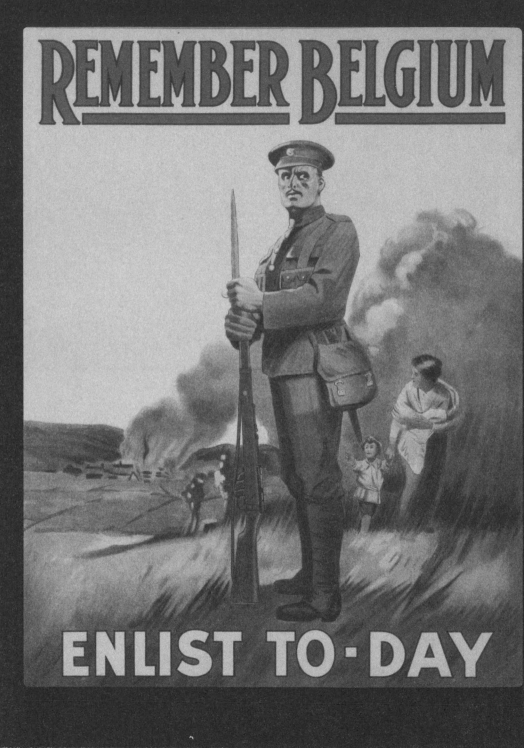

I
WAR BEGINS IN EUROPE

"Heir to Austrian Throne Assassinated; Wife by His Side
Also Shot to Death," blazed the headline in the *New York Tribune* on June 29,
1914. "Bullets from a . . . revolver in the hands of [a] . . . youth riddled the
heir apparent and his wife. . . . Another terrible chapter has thus been written into the tragic and romantic history of the House of Hapsburg [rulers
of Austria-Hungary]. . . . The flying bullets struck [Franz] Ferdinand full in
the face. . . . An instant later he . . . sank to the floor of the car in a heap."

The nineteen-year-old assassin was Gavrilo Princip, one of a group
of seven young men who planned to kill Franz Ferdinand. The shooting
happened in Sarajevo, the capital of Bosnia, but not the Bosnia on the map
today. Bosnia in 1914 was part of the Austro-Hungarian Empire, which was
a territory much larger than today's Austria. The empire also included what
is now Austria, Hungary, the Czech Republic, Slovakia, Slovenia, Croatia,

Germany invaded Belgium early in the war, violating its right to be neutral. Britain
joined in Belgium's defense, becoming one of the Allies. This 1915 British poster
encourages men to sign up for the army in order to protect innocent Belgians,
especially mothers and children.

and parts of Poland, Romania, Italy, and Ukraine. It ruled people speaking more than fifteen languages, including German, Hungarian, Czech, Polish, and Italian, as well as the southern Slavic languages. Each had some desire to be independent. There was a movement to unite all Slavic-speaking peoples within their own nation. This was a nationalist movement—supported by people who thought that those with the same language, culture, and history should be able to live in countries governed by themselves.

Princip and his partners were from Serbia, which at the time was a small, independent country whose people spoke a Slavic language. They wanted Bosnia to become part of Serbia. Serbia was a leader in the movement to free Slavic-speaking peoples from Austria-Hungary. Austria-Hungary, however, wanted to control Serbia, stop all nationalist dissent, and rule southeastern Europe. The assassination of Franz Ferdinand set the Austro-Hungarian Empire against Serbia. Many people believe this tense political situation was the start of World War I.

Did a war that came to involve the entire world—a war that involved armies from six continents—really start because one man was shot and killed? In fact, the countries of Europe had been rivals for hundreds of years. So when Princip attacked the Austro-Hungarian heir in Bosnia, there was already a long history of feuding and competition. Austria-Hungary wasn't alone in wanting to hold more territory and have more power. Britain, France, Russia, and Prussia (which became part of Germany), as well as Austria-Hungary, fought wars against one another during the nineteenth and early twentieth centuries. Russia fought Japan in the Russo-Japanese War of 1904–5, over control of land in China and Korea, and lost. Serbia was successful in two Balkan wars in southeastern Europe in 1912 and in 1913. (The "Balkans" is one name for the area in southeastern Europe that includes Serbia.) The first pushed the Turkish (Ottoman) Empire out of some of its European territory.

The shooting of Archduke Franz Ferdinand, heir to the Austro-Hungarian Empire, was the spark that set off World War I. Here he is shown with his wife, Sophie, killed at the same time, and their three children.

In the second, Serbia defeated Bulgaria, a relatively large country that was a rival for Slavic control.

The boundaries and names of countries were continually changing during this period. Germany, for example, did not become the country known today as Germany until 1871, when the German-speaking region of Prussia united with other German-speaking states to its south. Prussia was already an organized, powerful state. After Germany formed, the country not only built up its military forces but also began claiming colonies in Africa and the Pacific Ocean region. These included Togoland (now Ghana and Togo), the Cameroons (now Nigeria and Cameroon), German East Africa (now Tanzania), and Papua New Guinea. Germany was becoming an imperialistic nation—one

EUROPE, 1914

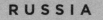
RUSSIA

SEA
OF
AZOV

CASPIAN SEA

LACK SEA

inople

**OTTOMAN
EMPIRE**

Nicosia

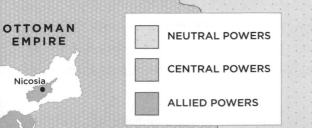
NEUTRAL POWERS

CENTRAL POWERS

ALLIED POWERS

This map shows the countries of Europe as they were in 1914. Austria and Hungary are part of one empire. Serbia sits below it. Most of Poland and Ukraine are part of Russia.

that sought control over other countries, through either political arrangements or force.

Germany's increasing power threatened Britain and France, already major imperialist countries. They had built up colonial empires of their own. Britain had control of countries around the world, including India, South Africa, and parts of China. Countries such as Canada and Australia governed themselves but continued to have close ties to Britain. They would provide military support if Britain ever went to war. France ruled colonies in Africa— including Morocco, Algeria, Tunisia, the Ivory Coast, and Senegal—and also in Southeast Asia—Laos, Cambodia, and Vietnam. Having colonies made a country more powerful. The colonies provided raw materials, trading partners, and land for immigrants from the home countries to settle and develop for farming and business. Colonies usually made the home countries richer.

In the early twentieth century, Britain had the largest empire and the largest navy in the world. The new Germany, itself an empire, challenged that supremacy. France had a long history of quarrels with Prussia and the other German territories. (In 1871, France lost a war to Prussia, which then took over parts of what had been French territory, Alsace and Lorraine. The French were still bitter about this loss in 1914.) Russia, which included what is now most of Poland, sat on Germany's eastern border; it was also Germany's rival in trying to influence the countries of eastern Europe. By the early twentieth century, Germany felt surrounded by potential enemies. (Britain did not border Germany on land but was superior on the seas off Germany's coast, although Germany was rapidly building up its own navy.) Germany decided to become the ally of Austria-Hungary—many people in Austria-Hungary spoke German—to balance the power of the other European countries. By the time it joined forces with Germany, the Austro-Hungarian Empire was fairly weak but still trying to control the different nationalities inside its borders. (Austria-Hungary did not have a colonial empire.)

The European countries signed treaties, some of them secret, agreeing to protect one another in case of war. By 1914, Russia had a treaty to defend Serbia. (Russians also spoke a Slavic language.) France had a defensive treaty with Russia and one with Britain. Britain had an agreement to defend Belgium, a small country that had stayed neutral through earlier wars. Austria-Hungary and Germany had a treaty to protect each other. Both countries had a treaty with Italy to protect them if they were attacked first; together the three formed what was known as "the Triple Alliance." Finally, Japan had an agreement to support Britain in case of war.

Few people expected that all these different treaties would be called upon at the same time or that all these countries would find themselves at war. But even ordinary people could sense that something was changing. "Germany endeavored to act as mediator in the Austro-Russian conflict," wrote the newspaper *Frankfurter Zeitung* on July 31, 1914. "In this effort she was supported by England, France, and Italy, because all these Powers, as is clearly shown by the attitude of their Governments and also by the expressions of public opinion, wished to avoid a great European war. But it appears that . . . we are at the beginning of that great European war of which there has been so much talk, but in which no one seriously believed until today."

The American novelist Edith Wharton noted that "Paris went on steadily about her mid-summer business of feeding, dressing, and amusing the great army of tourists who were the only invaders she had seen for half a century. All the while, every one knew that other work was going on. . . . Paris counted the minutes till the evening papers came. They said little or nothing except what every one was already declaring. . . . 'We don't want war.' . . . If diplomacy could still arrest the war, so much the better; no one in France wanted it. . . . But if war had to come, then the country, and every heart in it, was ready."

Three weeks after the assassination of Archduke Franz Ferdinand, Austria-Hungary demanded justice from Serbia. Serbia actually agreed to most of Austria's demands, but the empire declared war anyway on July 28, 1914. Like a tower of blocks falling one after another, the other countries followed.

Russia immediately began putting together a large army to aid Serbia and fight Austria-Hungary. On August 1, Germany (Austria-Hungary's ally) declared war on Russia. Germany then declared war on France (Russia's ally) on August 3. Later that same day, France declared war on Germany. On August 4, Germany marched into neutral Belgium on its way to Paris, pulling Britain into the war. Japan declared war on Germany on August 23. Austria-Hungary then declared war on Japan. Italy decided to stay neutral; this did not violate the country's treaty with Germany and Austria-Hungary, because the Italian government believed that Austria-Hungary had started the war. Even though Austria-Hungary was the first to declare war, Germany—with more military power and ambition—became the main enemy for France, Britain, and Russia and, eventually, for the United States.

When Sarah MacNaughtan, a Scotswoman who would later be an aid worker in France, arrived in London toward the end of August, she wrote in her diary: "Hardly anyone believed in the possibility of war until they came back from their August . . . Holiday visits and found soldiers saying good-bye to their families at the [train] stations. And even then there was an air of unreality about everything. . . . We saw women waving handkerchiefs to the men who went away, and holding up their babies to railway carriage windows to be kissed. . . . We were breathless, not with fear, but with astonishment."

Germany declared war on Russia on August 1, 1914, and war on France on August 3. Here hundreds of Germans cheer in front of the cathedral in Berlin when they hear the news.

People in the warring countries and observers like the United States expected the war to be a short one. Each side felt sure it would quickly win. In fact, everyone predicted that the soldiers would be home for Christmas. But instead, the war lasted from 1914 through 1918 and drew in countries around the world. Italy eventually joined on the side of the Allies—Britain, France, and Russia—in May 1915. Among the nations supporting the Allies were China, Greece, Portugal, Brazil, Guatemala, and Romania. Those who entered the war later on the side of the Allies were called "Associated powers." Japan and Portugal, for example, were Associated powers. The United States was as well. It preferred to be an "associate" rather than one of the main Allied powers, so that it would be completely independent from the British, French, and Russian governments in making military and diplomatic decisions.

Britain and France brought in troops from their colonies and former colonies to fight the war. Troops that supported the British included Cana-

These soldiers from India, one of Britain's colonies, fought with the British against the Germans. Both Britain and France used colonial troops in the war.

dians, Australians, New Zealanders, East Asian Indians, and South Africans. France had the help of troops from Senegal, Morocco, and its other African colonies. Not only did colonial troops fight in Europe, but the Allies fought Germany in Germany's African colonies. Germany provided support for the Ottoman Empire, which had success in battles against the British in Egypt but never completely controlled the country. It lost German East Africa to the Allies, but German forces continued to fight in parts of Africa until the end of the war. Japan protected Allied trade routes in the western Pacific Ocean and the Indian Ocean from the German navy and took over German colonies in the Pacific and East Asia.

Countries fighting on the side of Germany and Austria-Hungary included Bulgaria and Turkey. Turkey was the center of the Ottoman Empire, with territory in parts of Europe, North Africa, and the Middle East. Germany, Austria-Hungary, and/or Turkey fought Russian, British, and French forces in several territories and countries, including Iran, Iraq, Egypt, Palestine (parts of which are now Israel or are occupied by Israel), Syria, and southeastern Europe.

In April 1917, the United States joined on the side of the Allies. Almost all of America's fighting was in France, against the Germans. Americans fought Austria-Hungary only in support of Italy. The United States declared war on Austria-Hungary in December 1917, after that country had defeated the Italians at the Battle of Caporetto and Italy requested help from the Allies. The United States never declared war on the Ottoman Empire. American troops were also sent to Panama to protect the Panama Canal.

U.S. troops fought in Russia only after the Russian government was taken over by the Bolshevik party in the October Revolution of 1917, which led to the establishment of the Soviet Union. The Bolsheviks were communists who maintained that the people of a country should jointly own all property, such as farms and factories, and that they should share equally with one another.

In practice, communist governments did not allow much dissent or disagreement. The other Allies did not welcome the idea of communism in their own countries. The United States, for example, did not recognize the Soviet Union until many years after the war had ended.

The Allies were left with a new problem, however, when the Bolsheviks quit their war against Germany, signing a peace treaty in March 1918. Since the Allies were not sure that Germany would honor this peace—especially since there were a lot of weapons supplied by the Allies still in Russian territory—several Allied Countries, including the United States, sent troops to Russia.

Looking back at all these events, we realize now that World War I was neither short nor simple. But even so, when Archduke Franz Ferdinand was assassinated—even after war broke out between a few European countries in 1914—it would have been hard to imagine that over the next four years battles would rage in nearly every corner of the world.

American and other Allied troops fought in Russia after that country made peace with Germany. Here soldiers and sailors from many countries march in front of the Allied headquarters building in the Russian city of Vladivostok.

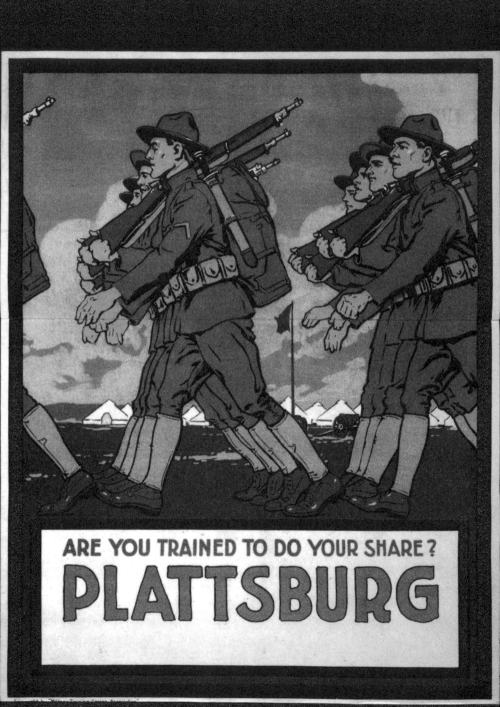

2

THE UNITED STATES STAYS NEUTRAL—OR DOES IT?

Although war began in Europe in 1914, the United States did not jump into the fight. The distance between the United States and Bosnia was about 5,500 miles. By plane today, it would take almost ten hours to fly from one country to the other. But there were no planes flying overseas then. People—including soldiers—traveled by ship across the Atlantic, then by truck, train, or horse- or mule-drawn vehicle, or by foot over the land to their destinations. Separated by an ocean from Europe, Americans (many of them immigrants from Europe) did not fear physical attack from the countries at war.

Because Americans came from so many countries, including the warring

Before the United States entered the war, some Americans believed the country should be prepared to fight by training young men at private military camps. The first took place in Plattsburgh, New York. Other Americans were pacifists who believed the United States should not go to war.

A British blockade prevented supplies, including food, from getting through to Germany. In 1916, the Berlin People's Kitchen served soup for eight cents a cup from a horse-drawn cart, offering German civilians at least one hot meal a day.

ones, President Woodrow Wilson declared that the United States would be "neutral in thought as well as in action." That meant it would support neither the Allied Countries nor the Central Powers. Many Americans were in favor of neutrality. As far back as 1776, when the United States proclaimed its independence from Britain, it had tried to stay out of European struggles. But the United States was not economically separate from the rest of the world. It traded with many countries, including some in South America and Asia, selling everything from agricultural products (wheat, cotton) and industrial products (steel, machinery) to raw materials (iron, coal). In 1913, the United

States accounted for a little more than one-tenth of the world's trade. American prosperity depended on the country's ability to sell products to other countries, especially Britain.

In August 1914, when World War I began in Europe, the U.S. government stated that Americans could not lend money to any of the warring countries. But the United States was suffering through a depression, and economic and political leaders realized that not trading with Europe would make the economy worse. In October 1914, Wilson gave permission for American banks to loan money to Britain, France, Germany, and other countries waging war. With borrowed money these countries could pay the United States for food, weapons, and other products. As a result, American businesses, banks, and industries began to profit from the war.

Although Wilson's decision did not keep Germany and the other Central Powers from also borrowing or trading with the United States, a British blockade of sea access to Germany did. Beginning early in 1915, the British prevented merchant ships carrying goods to Germany from getting through. Merchant ships carried all kinds of cargo, as well as passengers, and could carry weapons. Because Britain had the most powerful navy in the world, it was able to keep German ships from sailing out of German ports. It also laid down explosive mines in the Baltic Sea and the North Sea. If neutral ships—like those of the Americans—wanted to reach Germany, they had to have permission from Britain, which would tell them how to avoid the mines. Britain would not give this permission to neutral ships carrying any product that would help Germany win the war. Even food for civilians was considered helpful to Germany in war. This would have a great impact on civilian morale as the war continued. The winter of 1916–17 was called "Turnip Winter" in Germany because there was so little to eat. Fifteen-year-old Elfriede Kuhr's grandmother went to buy horsemeat at a butcher's shop in an east German town. Before she got inside, she fainted from hunger. The butcher drove her home. Elfriede and her younger brother were frightened by how weak and pale their grandmother looked.

The British blockade made Americans uneasy. Blocking neutral ships seemed to conflict with the international rules for warfare accepted by most countries in Europe. These rules had been drawn up at two international conferences to promote peace: the Hague Conventions of 1899 and 1907, both of which took place in the Netherlands. They called for the rights of merchant ships and all neutral ships to travel freely. Mines that could damage these ships should not be laid off enemy coasts.

The United States objected to the blockade but in the end accepted it. The country's biggest trading partner was Britain. Americans had far-reaching cultural and family ties, back to when they had been British colonists. President Wilson's mother had been born in Britain. On August 19, 1914, Wilson had told a British official that the two countries were "bound together by common principle and purpose."

Although the largest numbers of foreign-born immigrants in the United States were German—many of them sympathetic to Germany—German actions drew the most criticism. The German invasion of neutral Belgium upset many Americans. They viewed it as unfair, "a big dog pouncing on a little one." The American journalist Will Irwin observed that after "three days of the German army [in Belgium] . . . it seemed to me . . . that the whole world had turned into a gray machine of death—earth and air and sky."

Then, on February 4, 1915, Germany announced that the sea around Britain was a war zone and it would use submarines against merchant ships. German submarines were called "U-boats," after the German word *Unterseeboot* (meaning "undersea boat"). More modern in design than British submarines, they were Germany's special weapon. Small, easy to maneuver, and hard to

This drawing of the *Lusitania* appeared in the *New York Herald*. After the German torpedo struck, there was a second explosion inside the ship. No one is sure what caused it, but the *Lusitania* sank rapidly, in just eighteen minutes.

detect, they had already sunk several British cruisers by firing torpedoes. They would now go after all merchant ships because, the Germans said, British ships often disguised their origin by flying American or other neutral flags. They told the United States that every ship that sailed in the war zone would be in danger. This was a violation of the accepted international rules for warfare. The United States had accepted Britain's blockade against Germany. What would it do about German submarines attacking neutral ships without warning?

Germany did warn Americans not to sail on British ships. But before the United States reached a firm decision about how to react to the submarine threat, a U-boat torpedoed the British passenger ship *Lusitania* on May 7, 1915. Near the coast of Ireland, the ship sank in just eighteen minutes. Even the captain of the German submarine, Walther Schwieger, said later, "It was the most terrible sight I have ever seen. The ship was sinking with unbelievable rapidity and there was a terrible panic on its decks. Desperate people ran helplessly up and down while men and women jumped into the water and tried to swim to empty overturned lifeboats." Out of 1,962 passengers and crew, 785 passengers and 413 crew members died. Of those dead, 128 were Americans.

The United States was outraged. The loss of so many American lives seemed reason enough to go to war with Germany. In fact, people often link the sinking of the *Lusitania* to our entering World War I. But the United States did not declare war—not for another two full years. In the next few weeks, Wilson's government debated issues such as whether the German sinking of a passenger ship was worse than the British blockade, which kept food from German civilians. The Germans argued that the *Lusitania* had secretly been carrying weapons. It was later proved to have been carrying ammunition, but whether it carried explosives has been argued back and forth for a hundred years. In the end, the United States sent three notes of protest to Germany. The last said that our country would consider the torpedoing of passenger and merchant ships to be "deliberately unfriendly." After a ship called the *Arabic* went down in August, claiming two more American lives, Germany backed away from its decision to sink these kinds of ships.

What happened in the United States in the two years after the *Lusitania* was torpedoed, as the war in Europe continued? Americans showed no overwhelming support for one side or the other. German Americans often favored Germany, but immigrants and their descendants from Serbia, Bosnia, and other areas of southeastern Europe were against Austro-Hungarian control. Many Irish Americans were anti-British because Britain still controlled Ireland. In 1916, Britain fiercely suppressed an Irish rebellion for independence, creating more anger. Americans who were descended from Belgian, French, and British immigrants tended to have sympathy for the Allies. Neutrality suited a country made up of so many diverse peoples with diverse opinions. There were, however, Americans who felt they needed to join the fight right away. They enlisted in the British and Canadian armies and in the French Foreign Legion. In 1916, about forty American airplane pilots formed a flying squadron in France. They were called "the Lafayette Escadrille," named after the Marquis de Lafayette, a Frenchman who fought in the American Revolution.

There were two other groups of Americans, crossing ethnic lines, who were very vocal in their feelings about the war. One group was pacifist, while the other felt that the American military was not large enough or strong enough to fight a big war. This last group favored what was called "preparedness"—preparing the United States for possible war by building up its military strength. Former president Theodore Roosevelt was perhaps its most famous supporter. Roosevelt wanted "acceptance by the nation of the principle of universal, obligatory military training in time of peace, as a basis of universal, obligatory service in time of war." He thought every man—though definitely not women—should have to train in peacetime as well as serve in war.

Roosevelt and many other preparedness advocates wanted to immediately provide military training to civilians in private camps. In August 1915, young men gathered at one of these camps in Plattsburgh, New York. "In the present unprepared condition of the United States it would be possible for a first-class foreign power, once it gained control of the sea, to land an army of 450,000 men on the Eastern seaboard of the United States," Colonel Edward F. Glenn told the trainees. From there, this enemy power could "gain control of the important territory that lies between Portland, Me., and the capes of Virginia, and then gradually, perhaps quickly, move westward." This seemed extreme, but preparedness supporters believed anything could happen.

By 1916, more than 16,000 men had trained in camps in several states.

At this training camp for civilians in Plattsburgh, New York, young men were organized as if they were in the regular U.S. Army. Here Company K of the 4th Training Regiment takes a break from hiking to have a meal.

Many came from wealthy families and had good, often Ivy League, educations. They had the time and money to train and they had high ideals about defending the United States. But the movement had support from other kinds of Americans as well. In May 1916, 135,000 people marched for preparedness in New York City in a parade that lasted twelve hours. Three hundred fifty thousand preparedness supporters marched in ten different cities on June 3. Women as well as men marched in these parades, advocating for building up the U.S. military.

Two events helped the preparedness cause: the sinking of the *Lusitania* and the raiding of Columbus, New Mexico, by Pancho Villa on March 9, 1916. Villa was a general in the Mexican Revolution against the ruling powers in Mexico. His invasion into American territory—even though he didn't get very far—provoked fear that another country could attack our own. American troops spent the next nine months hunting unsuccessfully for Villa in Mexico. General John Pershing was in charge of these troops. He would go on to lead the American forces in World War I. President Wilson acknowledged the concern for preparedness by signing the National Defense Act in June to provide funding for expanding the U.S. Army.

Every event that alarmed preparedness supporters produced a different effect on another large group of Americans—pacifists. They were peace activists who were against all war. "We are a committee of American citizens formed to protest against the attempt to stampede this nation into a reckless program of military and naval expansion," announced a flyer prepared by the Anti-Preparedness Committee in 1915. "No danger of invasion threatens this country, and there is no excuse for hasty, ill-considered action."

Many women were involved in the peace movement. Fifteen hundred marched in the Woman's Peace Parade on August 29, 1914, less than a month after war broke out in Europe. They walked behind a white banner featuring a dove, down Fifth Avenue in New York City. "There were no bands; there was dead silence and the crowds watched the parade in the spirit of the marchers, with sympathy and approval," observed Oswald Garrison Villard, son of the march's organizer Fanny Garrison Villard. "The silence, the dignity, the black dresses of the marchers—those who did not have black dresses wore black arm bands—the solemnity of the crowds, all of these produced a profound effect on the beholders." Women demonstrated against war even though at this point most of them could not vote. Many of them also campaigned for the vote at the same time.

Some of these women formed the Woman's Peace Party. They were particularly against war as mothers who wanted to protect their children. "As women, we feel a peculiar moral passion of revolt against both the cruelty and

These American women, including the social activist Jane Addams, sailed to the Hague, in the Netherlands, to attend the 1915 International Congress of Women. The congress called for a peaceful end to World War I, to be brought about by diplomacy, not more fighting. More than a thousand women from twelve countries attended, including Germany and Austria-Hungary.

waste of war. As women, we are especially the custodians of the life of the ages. We will no longer consent to its reckless destruction," declared the party in January 1915. Jane Addams was its leader. She was an influential social worker and reformer and founder of the Hull House in Chicago, a settlement house that helped immigrants adjust to the United States.

Many proponents of peace came out of what was called "the Progressive Movement," which was active from about 1890 to 1920. Social workers, teachers, journalists, and some political figures were among those who believed that city and state government programs could improve the lives of all Americans, including the poor, immigrants, and African Americans. They wanted political leaders to be honest and not give jobs or benefits just to their friends and supporters. They were against monopolies—huge businesses that were the only suppliers of items such as oil, steel, or agricultural products. They sought antitrust laws to prevent these large corporations from accumulating too much power, so that smaller businesses could survive. They worked for—and succeeded at getting—merit tests for government workers that would not show favoritism.

Many progressives were socialists. (Some were not—including Theodore Roosevelt.) Socialists believed that government, not private individuals, should own factories, mines, railroads, and other businesses that produced critical goods. They thought that a country's economy should be set up to meet the needs of the public and not to make profits for a few people. Most socialists saw war as a way for big businesses to make money. War did not help the worker, who likely would be drafted and risk his life in battle and fight against the workers of other countries, who also would not benefit from it.

American businesses were already making a lot of money from the war in Europe, supplying the Allies with weapons, munitions, food, raw materials, steel, and other necessities. France and Britain had borrowed heavily from American banks. Therefore, the owners of industries and wealthy people were often on the side of preparedness and willing for the country to go to war. But Germany had backed away from its policy of torpedoing neutral ships, and there were no obvious threats against the United States. This was a big reason that the country did not join World War I during the first three years.

President Wilson believed that world peace was possible. On January 22, 1917, he urged the Allies and Central Powers to recognize "a peace without victory," based on "American principles" of democratic government, freedom to travel on the seas, and the equal rights of all countries. He saw himself as a mediator and broker of peace. But as the war went on, it seemed to him that only by taking part would the United States have enough power to influence the outcome.

Men slide down ropes to escape as their ship, torpedoed by a German U-boat in 1917, is sinking. One lifeboat is already pulling away.

In the winter of 1916–17, the German military persuaded Kaiser Wilhelm II that Germany should return to sinking Allied and neutral ships, this time without restrictions. The British blockade was starving Germany, and the country had more than one hundred submarines ready to go. They knew this policy would anger the Americans and possibly bring them into the war, but they believed they could beat the Allies first. They also believed that if the United States did enter the war, it would take months, if not years, for American troops to be prepared enough to make a difference. Germany let the United States know it would return to unrestricted submarine warfare on February 1, 1917.

Although the United States had kept diplomatic ties with Germany through 1916, Wilson broke off these ties on February 3, but still he did not ask Congress to declare war. By mid-February, he allowed American merchant ships to travel armed with defensive weapons. Then British spies intercepted a telegram from German Foreign Minister Arthur Zimmermann to the German ambassador to Mexico. They decoded the telegram and passed the contents on to the United States in late February. What became known as "the Zimmermann Telegram" proposed a German alliance with Mexico "on the following basis: make war together, make peace together, generous financial support and an understanding on our part that Mexico is to reconquer the lost territory in Texas, New Mexico, and Arizona."

In March 1917, German submarines sank three American merchant ships, with the loss of six American lives. This was nothing like the scale of the deaths on the *Lusitania*, but combined with the prospect of more losses and the attempt to engage Mexico in the war, the attacks pushed Wilson to ask Congress to declare war on April 2. A number of Americans, including some

Kaiser Wilhelm II (*center*) examines maps with two of his high-ranking generals, Paul von Hindenburg (*left*) and Erich Ludendorff (*right*). The German military supported the return to unrestricted attacks on Allied and neutral ships.

in Congress, still opposed entering the war. They felt that business and banking interests were pushing the United States to fight so that they could keep up profitable trading with the Allies. "It would seem plain that our resources are undiminished, our capital [money for investment] secure . . . that we are saving when others are losing, that we are living when others are dying, that with us the path is upward and with them it is in large measure downward. It seems certain that one result [of the war] is to be our own greater economic independence," proclaimed William C. Redfield, the U.S. secretary of commerce. Businesses and banks had an additional reason for wanting to enter the war. If the Allies lost the war—and this was a real possibility in the spring of 1917—Americans would never be repaid all the money they had loaned.

The journalist and prominent socialist John Reed asked: "How is it that the British can arbitrarily regulate our commerce with neutral nations, while we raise a howl whenever the Germans 'threaten to restrict our merchant ships going about their business?' Why does our Government insist that Americans should not be molested while traveling on Allied ships armed against submarines? We have shipped and are shipping vast quantities of war-materials to the Allies. . . . We have been strictly neutral toward the Teutonic [German and Austro-Hungarian] powers only. Hence the inevitable desperation of the [Germans]. . . . Hence this war we are on the brink of."

Nevertheless, Congress declared war on Germany. On April 4, the Senate voted 82 to 6, with 8 not voting. The House of Representatives voted 373 to 50 on April 6, the day the declaration was official. Nine representatives did not vote. Jeannette Rankin, the first woman elected to the House of Representatives, voted against going to war, joining 49 of her male colleagues.

Many Americans supported the war once the United States was in it. Even pacifists and socialists hoped for the best outcome: That, in a spirit of patriotism and resolve, the United States would become a stronger, better country, willing and able to take care of all its people. However, there was concern. The historian Frederick Lewis Allen wrote in the magazine *The Nation*, "The question is whether we can remain true to the American tradition in time of war. War necessitates organization, system, routine, and discipline. The choice is between efficiency and defeat. . . . We shall have to give up much of our economic freedom. We shall be delivered into the hands of officers and executives who put victory first and justice second." Allen reminded Americans that the United States could become another Germany—in becoming more military it might sacrifice democracy. "It would be an evil day for America," he declared, "if we threw overboard liberty to make room for efficiency."

3

THE UNITED STATES JOINS THE FIGHT

When the United States declared war on Germany, no one knew exactly how the military would proceed. Britain was some 3,400 miles away, and the battlefields of France even farther. "Good Lord! You're not going to send soldiers over there, are you?" said a surprised Senator Thomas S. Martin of Virginia when the War Department asked Congress for $3 billion ($55.5 billion in today's money) to start building and training a huge army. But President Wilson quickly decided that the country had to provide troops overseas for the war to be sure the Allies would win. He also wanted to play a large part in setting the terms of peace when it came. By the end of the war, more than 4 million men had served in the

This poster was created in 1917 for the Mayor's Committee for National Defense in New York, after the United States declared war on Germany. It encourages men to enlist in the army with their friends. Many family members and friends did join and were stationed together.

U.S. military—and 2 million of them had been shipped across the Atlantic Ocean to France.

About 127,000 troops were in the regular army when war was declared. An additional 80,000 were in the National Guard. (Each state has a National Guard force to protect it.) In addition, some 300,000 men volunteered, many of them in their late teens and twenties.

"We men, most of us young, were simply fascinated by the prospect of adventure and heroism," remembered William L. Langer. "Here was our one great chance for excitement and risk. We could not afford to pass it up." Others believed they were fighting to save democracy and for a more peaceful, stable future. "What actuated me most was to end all wars," said Bill Morgan, who dropped out of college to serve. Once in France, he was eager to get into battle. "It is all so thrilling and it never enters your head that you are the one that may be shot . . . it is such a tremendous thing to be taking part in—when you think that the ideals of the world are at stake."

But the majority of soldiers—2.7 million men—were drafted, or "conscripted." Congress passed the Selective Service Act, which took effect on May 18, 1917, calling for men between the ages of twenty-one and thirty to register with local "draft boards." These boards would then decide who would be "selected" for the military. Others would support the war by staying at home to work in industry and farming. "The whole nation must be a team, in which each man shall play the part for which he is best fitted," said Wilson in a presidential proclamation on May 28. "To this end, Congress has provided that the nation shall be organized for war by selection; that each man shall be classified for service in the place to which it shall best serve the general good to call him."

Draft boards usually did not draft men if they were married and provided the only means of support of their families. Some men were conscientious

Many American women worked to recruit new soldiers. This snapshot of three recruiters, a doughboy, and a chauffeur appeared in the *Sunday Oregonian* newspaper on May 20, 1917, a little more than a month after war was declared.

objectors (COs). These included Quakers, Jehovah's Witnesses, and Menno-nites, who would not kill because of their religion. They also included those who would not fight for personal and political reasons—pacifists—who thought that any war was wrong. Some COs were drafted anyway. Others were assigned nonmilitary duties in the army but not forced into combat. One of these who served wrote that he was "[s]till strongly against compulsory military service excepting case of actual invasion. Would like to see all armies completely abolished." Nonetheless, he, like many conscientious objectors, was a member of the medical corps, a very dangerous job that involved carry-ing wounded soldiers from the battlefield, often under fire.

Men who were drafted with little or no military experience suddenly found themselves in training camps or on their way to Europe. "Soldiering meant a complete new life for all of us," said Corporal Paul Murphy, "and it was pretty hard to become adjusted to taking orders and having your whole life regulated by authority other than your own."

The U.S. armed forces sent to Europe, including soldiers and marines, were known as "the American Expeditionary Force" (AEF). American infantry or foot soldiers (as opposed to cavalry soldiers on horseback) were nicknamed "doughboys." There are several theories about how the nickname started, most going back to the mid-nineteenth century. One is that the ball-shaped buttons on infantry uniforms looked like dumplings, or dough-boys. Another is that the white clay used to polish uniforms and belts turned dough-like in the rain. Yet another is that when the United States had fought against Mexico in 1848, soldiers were said to kick up desert dust as they marched, which made them look like adobe clay buildings. None of these theories are proven.

All American soldiers and marines sent to Europe had one thing in common: They crossed the Atlantic Ocean by ship. By the summer of 1917, military ships protected the troop ships from German submarine attack. They also protected passenger ships and merchant ships with weapons and goods

The "submarine chaser" (*foreground*) was a kind of ship, first developed in the United States during World War I, designed to combat U-boats. Here is one at Brest, France, along with two larger ships that might need its protection.

These American soldiers are on their way to France in 1917. Every American who battled in the war had to cross the Atlantic Ocean by ship.

destined for the Allies, which usually sailed in convoys. (A "convoy" was a group of nonmilitary ships traveling with an escort of navy ships, whether those of the U.S. Navy or the ships of another Ally.) More than 1,100,000 American men sailed on troop ships between May 1917 and November 1918. Only 637 died because their ships were torpedoed. In February 1918, the ship *Tuscania* sank after being hit by a German torpedo. Other ships in the convoy were able to rescue 2,187 of the 2,397 troops who would otherwise have drowned.

Convoy duty was one of several jobs assigned to the U.S. Navy. Though not as large as the army's forces, the navy had some 81,000 sailors serving during World War I, aboard 370 American ships. Because the United States did not have enough ships available when it entered the war, many of its troops traveled on British ships. American naval men searched the English Channel and the North Sea (bordering Germany) for German submarines. They also patrolled off the East Coast of the United States, on the lookout for subs.

America's fighting men sailed in different models of ships, some big, some smaller, including destroyers, which were very fast and agile. Destroyers did not sit deep in the water, so torpedoes launched by submarines usually passed below them without harm. However, a destroyer often rolled (leaned heavily from side to side) because it rode higher in the water than larger ships. This caused the deck to be at an angle at which anything that was not fastened could slide into the sea. Tilford Irving Harding described one night on the USS *DeKalb*: "54 degrees was a common angle for the *DeKalb* to take." The ship's doctor and his assistants sometimes "clawed their way up and down among the injured men, helping to get the . . . [injured] soldiers [the ship carried] back into their bunks from which the crazy lurchings of the ship had dumped the wounded men. One wave smashed a deck-house in and the next one slammed what was left of it overboard. Life boats were stove in, funnels were bent."

Sailors faced other kinds of danger. U.S. Navy ships, along with the British, laid mines in the North Sea, along a stretch of 230 miles. Although there to explode German ships, the Allied ships carrying the mines were also in danger of exploding. "We made a barrage of mines off the Norway Coast to Scotland, with from five to eight ships abreast, each dropping a mine every five to 12 seconds," said Lester T. Lee, who served on the USS *Dizzy Quinne*. "At first it was exciting, but soon became real work; loading mines, . . . and in the bunkers the [coal] dust is so thick you had to put [a] handkerchief over your mouth to get your breath. . . . Our only danger was . . . German mines laid by subs in front of us, our own mines coming [loose] . . . and floating in our path, or collisions in the fog." Lee concluded, "Believe me, we realize[d] we were not at home."

Once American soldiers and marines reached Europe, they had different jobs. About 800,000 AEF men provided support services, like transporting supplies and building roads. Some 1.2 million experienced battle. They were all commanded by General John J. Pershing. He upheld Wilson's desire to keep the AEF separate and independent, rather than have it assigned to existing British and French armies, which would have put it under the command of British and French officers.

Americans believed the French and British way of fighting got too many soldiers killed. (In the end, Americans had to accept some of these tactics, simply because of the condition of the territory they were fighting in.) Early in the war, by October 1914, the warring countries had developed a new style of combat. French and British soldiers had stopped the further advance of German soldiers into France. But British and French troops were not able to push the Germans back. Instead, each side literally dug in. Using shovels and picks, they dug deep, long, narrow holes called "trenches." Soldiers could shelter there from the enemy's weapons.

Allied trenches were usually about seven feet deep and six feet wide. German trenches were as deep as twelve feet. Sandbags, wire mesh, bunches of twigs, and wooden frames propped up the trench walls. Wooden boards were used for floors. The Germans were digging on higher ground; the Allies, nearer to water underground, often found their trenches flooded, and the soldiers were prone to diseases like trench foot, which caused swelling and open sores. Some German trenches even had electricity and telephone lines, which the Allies' trenches did not. American Charles Senay later described his trench as "very old and deep. . . . There was a sea of rusted barbed wire between the lines. My dugout was . . . shored and lined with

Soldiers in France repair a frontline trench after a bomb explosion. They are fifty yards from the German trenches. This photograph was taken during the filming of a silent movie, *Hearts of the World*, by noted American producer and director D. W. Griffith. He was asked by the British government to make the film to persuade Americans to support the war. It was shown in American theaters.

wood. Myriads of brown rats swarmed behind the woodwork. At night, they would fight for any food scraps on the floor."

The trenches formed a giant network, hundreds of miles long, that was connected by smaller trenches that covered miles of ground. They marked out the Western Front—the battle line between Allies and Germans in Western Europe. This line was not straight; the trenches were dug in zigzag patterns to make them easier to defend. Soldiers were relatively safe in the trenches, where artillery shells passed over their heads. "The shells used to come pretty often," remembered Private Anthony Pierro. "Shells are coming your way and you don't know where to duck." Soldiers were warned by the sound. "They used to make a whistle when the shell was flying," continued Pierro. "They went *weeeeee, ba-BOOM!* when it hit the ground and exploded." Having soldiers protected by the trenches is one reason World War I lasted so long.

But in order to advance, the armies had to face each other on open ground. The battleground between the two lines of trenches was called "No Man's Land." This was an open space, sometimes only fifteen yards wide, between the two sides. It was filled with shell holes and barbed wire—and dying and dead soldiers. "The horror of the thing outruns all imagination," wrote Walter Hines Page, the U.S. ambassador to Britain, to President Wilson. "[M]en marched into the trenches to as certain slaughter as cattle. . . . There's nothing of the old 'glory' of war—the charge, the yell, the music, the clash, and the giving way of one side or of the other. . . . Just plain, beastly butchery of men in such numbers as were never before killed in battle in so short a time."

There was little cover for soldiers as they went "over the top"—out of the trenches into open combat. Private Peter Schaming Jr., who dropped out of high school to enlist in the New York National Guard, described his experience in September 1918 in a letter to his parents: "I will try to tell you the best way I can about the drive we made. . . . [W]e were brought out into 'No Man's Land' about two hundred yards in front of our first line. . . . [W]e got into a little shell hole for cover on account of the flying shrapnel [pieces of metal]. All at once every [Allied] gun in back of us opens up fire [on the Germans]. With that . . . [the] German opens up his artillery. . . . The shells were so close at times that they had us buried with dirt. . . . The Corporal sticks his head up and gets hit with shrapnel so we bandaged him up . . . and leave him there in the shell hole. . . . [W]e get up [to the German's front line] and killed all the Germans we seen. . . . When your back was turned they would let loose with a machine gun. So it was a case of kill them before they

German troops lie dead in a trench in the La Bassée region of France. No date is given.
It is estimated that approximately 1,770,000 German soldiers lost their lives in World War I.

get you. . . . [W]e came back to our old front line to get some more shells
. . . but the Major there wouldn't let us go back because everybody going up
there was killed by machine gun fire. . . . I just heard now my Seargent was
dead. The Infantry company that I went over the top with came back with
four men. . . ."

The number of losses from these assaults was enormous. In the Battle
of the Somme, for example, which lasted four and a half months (July–
November 1916), 200,000 French, 400,000 British, and 650,000 German
soldiers were killed or wounded. President Wilson and General Pershing—
and the American public—did not want to see Americans thrown into open
combat, only to be killed in massive numbers like these.

As the war progressed, some American divisions did come under British or French command, but the majority remained independent and under American control. The first soldiers from the United States reached France in June 1917. It wasn't until 1918, however, that they went on the attack against the German army. After three days of fighting (May 28–31) at Cantigny, France, they took over high ground held by the Germans, making it easier to spot the enemy's next moves. The exhausted soldiers who returned from the battle "could only stagger back, hollow-eyed with sunken cheeks, and if one stopped for a moment he would fall asleep," recalled Colonel Hanson Ely. But in late May, after Russia quit the war, the German army was able to move

These members of the American Medical Corps carry an injured soldier from battle in Vaux, France, on July 22, 1918. Medics, including conscientious objectors who would not carry arms, operated under fire and were essential to saving the lives of doughboys.

Soldiers take cover as an artillery shell explodes near their trench. This photograph was taken near Reims, at Fort de la Pompelle, one in a line of defensive forts built by the French in the early 1880s after the loss to Germany during the Franco-Prussian War of 1870.

within forty miles of Paris. One million people deserted the city in fear. At Château-Thierry, U.S. Marines helped stop the German advance. The loss of Paris would have been a disaster for the French and for the Allies. American support did not win the battle, but it raised the Allies' spirits at a time when morale was very low and victory important.

In the fall of 1917, before the battle at Cantigny, the Italian army had suffered a major defeat against the Germans and Austro-Hungarians at the Battle of Caporetto. In late October, the Italian government asked the Allies for help. The British and French sent troops. The U.S. Army did not have troops to send right away, but Americans volunteered as ambulance drivers—including the writer Ernest Hemingway. The United States formally declared war on Austria-Hungary in December 1917. In July 1918, the American 332nd Infantry Regiment arrived in Italy, where it fought well. The United States also supplied airplane pilots for bombing missions.

At the beginning of June 1918, American soldiers and marines had begun a three-week fight in Belleau Wood, a thick French forest that hid the German positions. To reach them, the Americans had to cross a wide-open wheat field. "They started us in waves towards the . . . Woods," said Private Eugene Lee. It was almost like playing a game of leap frog. "In four waves—we'd go along and jump the first wave as they go so far, then the next wave, they kept doing that until we reached the woods up there. . . . We kept going so far, and then you'd lie down, and the next wave would come in back of them, jump each one until they . . . got in the woods, fighting." First the Americans won Belleau Wood from the Germans, then the Germans counterattacked and took it back. Command of the woods changed twelve times before, on June 26, the Americans could say with certainty that they had won. What they lost were almost 9,800 casualties, 1,811 of whom were dead.

American soldiers of the Regimental Headquarters Company, 23rd Infantry, fire a 37mm gun during an advance against German positions in the Argonne Forest. The Argonne was one of the last places where Americans fought in France.

In the summer of 1918, the United States sent troops to Russia—to Siberia and the port city of Vladivostok on the Pacific coast. The Bolshevik (Communist) Russian government had already signed a peace treaty with Germany, the Treaty of Brest-Litovsk. The Allies were afraid that Germany might seize the stock of weapons the Allies had supplied to Russia. They went in with the support of the Communist government. But the situation was complicated. Many Russians were not happy with the Bolshevik revolution. Many officers of the old Russian army and other anti-Communists (called "the Whites") began fighting to overthrow the Bolsheviks ("the Reds"). The Allies, including the United States, got caught up in the civil war on the side of the Whites. However, by 1919, with little progress made, most of the Allied troops had withdrawn. The United States left in 1920.

In France, as American troops arrived in Russia, the Aisne-Marne offensive began in mid-July 1918. Three hundred ten thousand American troops were put under French command. On July 18, the U.S. Third Division again and again stopped German attacks on the Marne River. They earned the nickname "the Rock of the Marne." The Americans helped win this campaign because by now there were so many of them in France, a substantial number of whom were better trained through real war experience. About 30,000 Americans a day were arriving by ship. German Chancellor Georg von Hertling noticed the number of U.S. reinforcements. "On the 18th [of July] even the most optimistic among us [German leaders] knew that all was lost. The history of the world was played out in three days."

But although the German government was uncertain, the German military did not believe it had completely lost the war. It kept fighting. The Germans had been stationed in what was called "the Saint-Mihiel salient"—a large bulge of German-held land that jutted out into French territory. At Saint-Mihiel, as the Allies attacked, they moved through darkness so deep they could not see one another but stayed together only by touching the packs of the soldiers ahead of them. When Eugene Kennedy came over a hill, he "saw a sight which I shall never forget. It was zero hour [1:00 a.m.] and in one instant the entire front as far as the eye could reach in either direction was a sheet of flame, while the heavy artillery made the earth quake." The flames came from a new German weapon, a flamethrower that shot out streams of fire. Nevertheless, on September 12, approximately 500,000 American and 100,000 French troops drove the Germans back fifteen miles from their frontline position.

Meanwhile, a deadly flu epidemic known as "Spanish influenza" was sweeping around the world. In Europe it killed tens of thousands of civilians, and also soldiers. From September through November nearly 100,000 American soldiers became sick, and about 10,000 died. Whether from battle or disease, "[e]verything is overflowing with patients," wrote an army surgeon. "Our divisions are being shot up; the wards are full of machine-gun wounds. There is rain, mud, 'flu,' and pneumonia. . . . In one night I had 60 deaths." Between May and November, 60,000 people in the U.S. military died. The flu epidemic continued into 1919.

The last big battles the Americans fought alongside the French army took place at the Meuse River and the Argonne Forest from September to November 1918. The fighting lasted forty-seven days. The German army fought back fiercely. The Germans were in position on higher ground and could observe American troops advancing and cut them down with machine-gun fire. Overcrowding of supply vehicles behind the lines caused tremendous traffic jams, and supplies could not get through. Some days it was hard to see in the foggy weather. Most of the American soldiers had received little training in this type of warfare and had no battlefield experience. In early October, German soldiers trapped one unit for five days, preventing them from getting food. This unit became known as "the Lost Battalion." By the time it was rescued, 70 percent of the soldiers had been either killed or wounded. Despite this push by the Germans, the end was drawing near. The German government sked President Wilson, and later the other Allies, for an armistice—a stop in the war.

The armistice was declared on November 11, 1918. An American volunteer working in France described it in her diary as a "memorable day in history of all world. At 11:00 a.m., fighting between Germany and Allies ceased. . . . French [people] decorated with flags. Left office early. Big parade and celebrating that night. [City Hall] & Palace of Justice were lit up. Fireworks were displayed and people made merry. . . . Went with . . . bunch of girls to see the celebrations. Beaucoup fun. 'FINIS LE GUERRE' [Much fun. End of the War]."

"You cannot imagine the goings on any more than I can describe it," W. H. Lefrancis wrote from Newark, New Jersey, on the day of the armistice. "It started at 4 o'clock this morning with the blowing of every factory whistle, the ringing of all the church bells, some horseman came through the street long before daylight, with a cornet, sounding the revelie, and then played the *Star Spangled Banner.*"

The United States celebrates those who served in all our country's wars with a national holiday, Veterans Day. It is always celebrated on November 11, in remembrance of the end of the first great war of the twentieth century, World War I.

The Battery D gun crew of the 105th Artillery raises the American flag after the last shot of the war was fired, as the armistice took effect. This photograph was taken near Etraye, France.

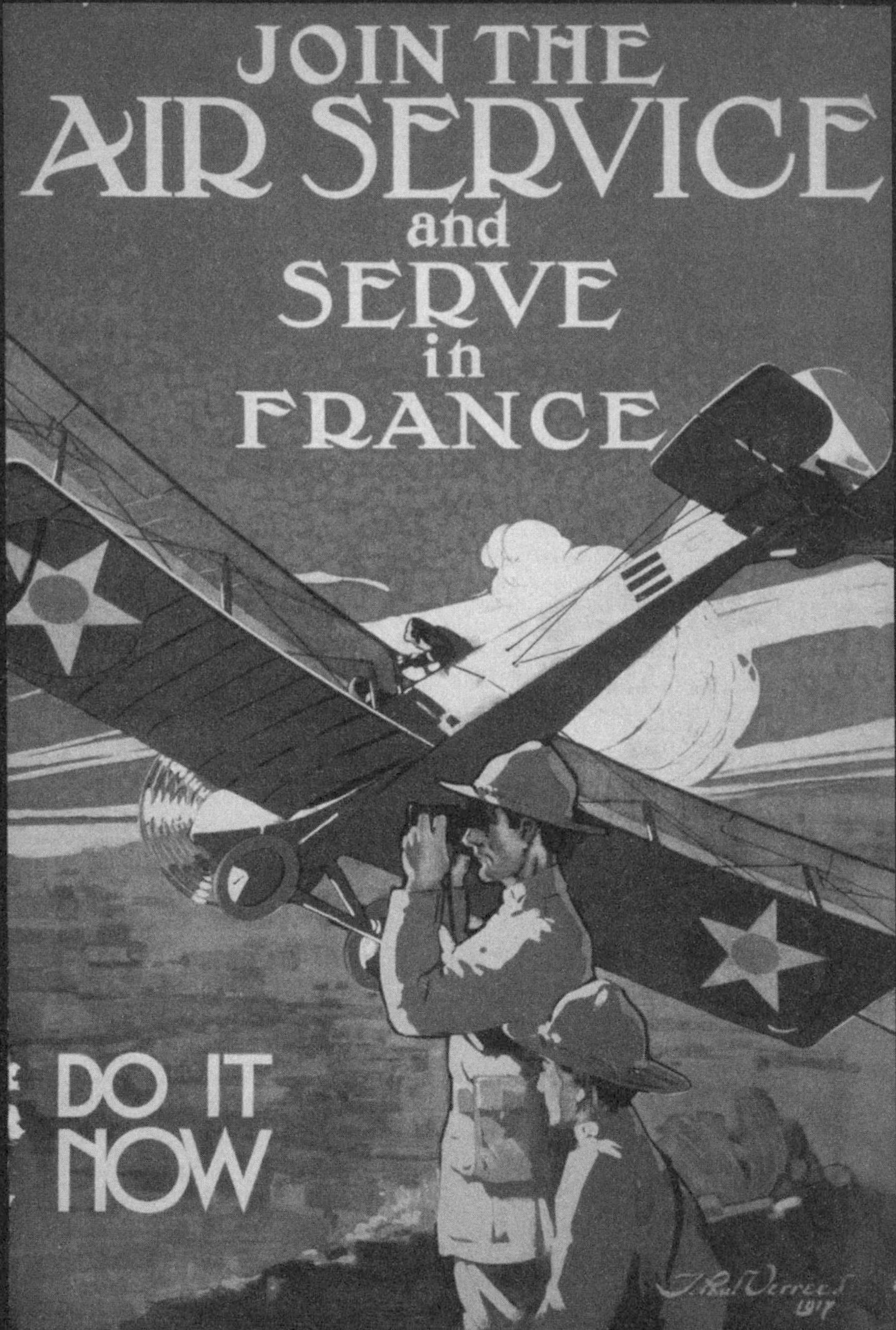
JOIN THE
AIR SERVICE
and
SERVE
in
FRANCE
DO IT
NOW
1917

4
NEW AND IMPROVED WEAPONS

Before World War I, battles had pitted soldier against soldier. Lines of infantry—soldiers on foot—from opposing sides would move toward each other. Armed with rifles, they would shoot an enemy or run him through with a bayonet. Cavalry—soldiers on horseback—would follow, their horses diving into combat with the enemy's cavalry, swiping with swords and sabers to bring down the enemy's horses and men. There were cannons and other artillery—large guns that stood in place, manned by more than one soldier—that fired from a distance. Their ammunition could kill several troops at a time or leave large holes in the ground. But most fighting was up close, man to man. Artillery was not powerful enough to wipe out assaults by hundreds of soldiers.

World War I was the first war where airplanes were used extensively. This 1917 poster urges Americans to join the air service. During the war, pilots and crew were part of the U.S. Army. A separate U.S. Air Force was not formed until 1947, after the Second World War.

All that changed during the course of World War I. At the advent of the war, soldiers of the Allied Countries and Central Powers were still charging one another. But bigger and better weapons could shoot down many men before they could take on each other singly. "Those who knew the great [European] armies of the pre-war days would hardly recognize them now," declared a 1917 article in *Hearst's Sunday American*. "Everything has changed—uniforms, weapons, methods, tactics. Experience has shown that almost all our pre-conceived ideas were wrong. . . . Cavalry have played no role on the western front for nearly two years." Older artillery—weapons such as cannons—used in the field had to be "reinforced by new giant artillery."

The cavalry still used some horses, but horses were also important for other jobs. More reliable than vehicles for getting through mud, they hauled much of the war's artillery. They transported supplies and carried the wounded. The British alone used half a million horses. Most of these were shipped from the United States, which sent 1,000 a day. Horses could be killed as easily as soldiers. At the Battle of Verdun in 1916, as many as 7,000 horses were killed in one day alone by French and German shells. Horses also died from harsh weather and working conditions.

But as *Hearst's Sunday American* pointed out, it was not in the cavalry but "in the infantry . . . that you see the greatest changes. The average person's idea of an infantry battalion is that of a thousand men armed with rifles and bayonets who have little to do on their own responsibility except to obey orders of their officers and carry a ghastly weight [of equipment] long distances on their backs. . . . Every infantryman is now a highly trained specialist who has a particular job to perform in attack and defense, and who requires at least a year's hard training to perfect him."

After the first few months of the war, soldiers began to spend much more time in the trenches than they did in direct attack. As harsh as life in

Once the pride of traditional armies, the cavalry became less important during World War I, although such units still existed. These British cavalrymen are passing through the ruined village of Caulaincourt on April 21, 1917. It was more common to use horses to transport weapons and supplies.

the trenches was, they offered the best protection from the deadly weapons developed between 1914 and 1917, when the United States entered the war.

Field guns shot out millions of shells during the war. Bullets were solid metal; shells were hollow cylinders filled with various kinds of explosives that made a big impact on landing. They came in all sizes. During the first Battle of the Marne in 1914, French field guns fired shells three inches in diameter. A battery of field guns could cover ten acres of land in less than fifty seconds without approaching the enemy. In five days they had fired 432,000 shells.

Soldiers could tell when a shell was heading toward them. "There was a sound like the roar of an express train, coming nearer at tremendous speed with a loud singing, wailing noise," an American Red Cross volunteer described the experience in 1916. "It kept coming and coming and I wondered when it would ever burst. Then when it seemed right on top of us, it did, with a shattering crash that made the earth tremble. It was terrible. The concussion felt like a blow in the face, the stomach and all over; it was like being struck unexpectedly by a huge wave in the ocean." The Red Cross volunteer was not hurt, but the shell left a crater in the earth "as big as a small room."

It was exactly this kind of fighting power—killing tens of thousands of men in the first weeks of the war—that led to trench warfare. On November 2, 1917, "[a]t three o'clock in the morning the Germans turned loose . . . several thousand shells," recalled U.S. Corporal Frank Coffman. "[T]he only thing that prevented our platoon from being entirely wiped out was the fact that our trenches were deep, and the ground soft and muddy with no loose stones." Nevertheless, the firing went on for forty-five minutes. Then the Germans fired above the frontline soldiers to keep support troops from advancing. "[T]wo hundred and forty [Germans] . . . hopped down on us," continued Coffman. "They had crawled up to our [barbed] wire under cover of their barrage and the moment it lifted were right on top of us."

Living with the sounds and vibrations of shells could cause "shell shock"—similar to what is now called "post-traumatic stress disorder" (PTSD). At first, this was thought to be caused by the physical force of the blast. Many of the victims, however, had no visible wounds. By 1917, doctors realized that shell shock was a breakdown of the mind caused by constant stress, even if the soldier was not physically injured. Harvey Cushing, a U.S. Army field surgeon, described one patient he met in France: "twenty-four years old, a clean-cut, fair-haired young fellow, of medium height and well built. . . . Apart from a couple of minor wounds (including burns from mustard gas) he was physically uninjured when he left the front . . . but he was suffering from severe visual and motor disturbance."

American soldiers surround a 155mm field gun. It fired shells that are a little more than six inches in diameter, which are lined up next to the gun. Exploding shells made loud noises and caused vibrations. Soldiers exposed to many explosions sometimes developed "shell shock," or post-traumatic stress disorder.

At the patient's first "real battle" in July 1918, all the officers above him were killed or wounded. He was put in charge. He was told to take a town from the Germans The town was won and lost nine times over the course of five days. He served as messenger and medical officer for his troops. Then he "was quite badly stunned by a high-explosive fragment which struck his helmet—like getting hit in the temple with a pitched baseball. . . . [He] was shaking and stammering and even found it difficult to sit down. . . . [He was] suffering from a severe headache, heard whistling in his ears, felt dizzy. . . . His memories became incoherent." The patient wanted to go back to the front lines but couldn't. Dr. Cushing diagnosed him as having "psychoneurosis in line of duty."

Different versions of shell shock are now common in every war. During

World War I the condition was treated with rest. Some shell shock victims were able to return to the front. Others did not recover quickly and needed extensive stays in psychiatric hospitals. Some did not recover at all.

Bullets fired from machine guns also terrorized World War I soldiers. Machine guns had been invented in the nineteenth century. A team of men, not an individual soldier, was needed to operate one. Because machine guns were heavy and difficult to move from place to place, they were not used a lot at the beginning of the war. But the Germans soon realized the guns would be excellent for defense, for cutting down rows of advancing soldiers. A soldier with a rifle could shoot fifteen accurate rounds of bullets a minute; a machine gun could shoot hundreds of rounds in the same amount of time. As the war progressed, machine guns on both sides became easier to use and more reliable.

U.S. Corporal Robert L. King was "assigned to a machine gun company.... We've been taught how to kill the Germans and we sure ought to get some of them with these machine guns for they shoot 600 times a minute. It takes two men to feed in the bullets, we are not supposed to get in the trenches with the infantry but [stay] slightly to the rear, for we shoot over the infantry's heads. We are stationed at both ends of the trenches."

Germans designed the first submachine gun that was easy to use. While the machine gun stayed in one location, the submachine gun could be carried by individual soldiers. It was able to fire multiple rounds per minute and had far more firepower than a rifle.

The automatic rifle, a weapon between the rifle and machine gun, was also faster to fire than a regular rifle. The French army used it to create "walking fire," a line of soldiers marching forward and shooting at the enemy at the same time. The Americans introduced the Browning automatic rifle. The first shipment arrived in France in the summer of 1918. These rifles were "highly praised," said a U.S. government report. They endured "hard usage, being on the front for days at a time in the rain and when the gunners had little opportunity to clean them, they invariably functioned well."

Many of the weapons in World War I grew out of simpler versions from earlier times. Some form of hand grenade—basically an empty container filled with gun powder—had been used since the fifteenth century. The grenade might be filled with stones or metal. There was a fuse attached—a kind of string that could be lit with fire at one end. After a soldier lit the fuse, he threw it at the enemy. When the flame reached the end of the fuse, the grenade exploded. Flying metal parts or stones could wound and kill people. Hand grenades were dangerous to use, because they could go off accidentally. An English engineer invented a relatively safe grenade in 1915. It had a pin that

Three soldiers of the 101st Field Artillery fire an antiaircraft machine gun at a German observation airplane. Ordinary rifles could shoot fifteen rounds of bullets a minute. A machine gun could shoot 600 rounds in that time.

was pulled for firing—a version of today's grenades. It could also be aimed more accurately. Millions of these were used in World War I by both the Allies and the Germans. They were often dropped into trenches and were deadly to anyone near them when they exploded.

Flamethrowers—*Flammenwerfers* in German—also developed first in Germany. A version that could be carried like a backpack, with a hose for shooting out a stream of flammable liquid (such as gasoline), appeared in 1910. The German army first used flamethrowers in a battle in 1915. British Captain F. C. Hitchcock remembered, "The defenders of . . . [his] sector had lost few men from actual burns, but the demoralising element was very great. We were instructed to aim at those who carried the flame spraying device. . . . It was reported that a . . . [German with a flamethrower] hit by a bullet blew up with a colossal burst." Eventually there were both knapsack flamethrowers and large ones fired from field artillery, which shot out containers filled with flaming fuel. The way to fight an attack, said Hitchcock, was to use "rapid fire and machine gun fire. As the flames shot forward, they created a smoke screen, so we realised we would have to fire 'into the brown' [smoke]."

The French army was the first to use gas—a form of tear gas—in August 1914. The German army next used it against the Russian army in January 1915. This was not deadly, but it irritated soldiers' eyes. Cold weather made the gas less effective, so it did not have a big impact on the Russians, who were often battling in an icy environment. In April 1915, the Germans used chlorine gas against the Allies at the second battle of Ypres in Belgium. Canadian soldier A. T. Hunter saw a "queer greenish-yellow fog that seemed strangely out of place in the bright atmosphere of that clear April day." The fog "paused, gathered itself like a wave and ponderously lapped over into the trenches. Then passive curiosity turned to active torment—a burning sensation in the head, red-hot needles in the lungs, the throat seized as by a stran-

These soldiers are learning to use gas masks at a training camp at Fort Dix, New Jersey, before they are sent overseas. Gas masks could prevent troops from breathing in chlorine or phosgene gas that damaged lungs. But they could not protect against mustard gas, which passed through skin—and even through clothing and boots—into the body, affecting breathing and often causing temporary blindness.

gler. Many fell and died on the spot." Chlorine gas attacked the lungs so that soldiers could not breathe. Later, phosgene gas, which also damaged the lungs, was added to chlorine.

The Allies too used gas as a weapon. The British used chlorine gas in September 1915 at the Battle of Loos in France. By 1918, 25 percent of the shells launched on the European front by both sides held some kind of gas. The Germans relied on gas the most. The French used about half of what the Germans did, and the British about one-third. Wearing a gas mask worked well to protect soldiers against chlorine and phosgene gas, and many styles were developed. Soon every soldier at the front carried one. There were also gas masks designed for horses and dogs. "Gas travels quickly, so you must not lose any time [putting on your mask]; you generally have about eighteen or twenty seconds in which to adjust your gas helmet," wrote Arthur Empey, an American who joined the British army before the United States entered the war. "A gas helmet is made of cloth, treated with chemicals. There are two windows, or glass eyes . . . through which you can see. Inside there is a rubber-covered tube, which goes in the mouth. You breathe through your nose; the gas, passing through the cloth helmet, is neutralized by the action of the chemicals."

This heavy British tank moves toward a bridge across the Somme River. The Somme Offensive, when French and British troops attacked German troops, began on July 1, 1916. It was one of the most deadly fights in any war. Tanks were not effective at the Somme, but they proved successful in later battles.

But gas masks did not offer protection against mustard gas, which was first used in 1917. Mustard gas could enter the body directly through exposed skin. It could even pass through clothes and heavy boots. Mustard gas dried out the tiny network of tubes in the lungs, making it painful to breathe. It caused blindness, vomiting, blisters, and bleeding. It actually caused relatively few deaths; only 2 to 3 percent of soldiers affected with mustard gas died. However, many were put out of action for days or weeks. While soldiers recovered from the symptoms of mustard gas, they could not fight.

Gas also frightened soldiers in a way that even the most dangerous artillery did not. Except for chlorine gas, it was invisible. Panic could spread if gas was in an area. Many soldiers complained of symptoms even though they had not actually been gassed. And all gases were dangerous weapons to use, even for the attacker. If the wind changed direction, they could affect one's own soldiers, not the enemy. The Americans, who produced gas for the British and French, did not use much gas themselves, partly for that reason.

Tanks were another weapon introduced in World War I. They were basically farm tractors covered with iron to protect the soldiers inside as they moved across almost any kind of land—open, hilly, muddy, covered with trees or crisscrossed with barbed wire. They also drove over trenches and stopped machine-gun shells. But they were heavy, often weighing more than thirty tons, and they moved slowly—about two and a half to three and a half miles an hour, the speed of a brisk walk. American soldier George Noble Irwin left a memoir for his son describing what it was like to be in one. "Life in the Mark V [tank] was very unpleasant, the air contaminated from poorly ventilated gases of carbon monoxide and cordite fumes. Loud beyond belief with temperatures reaching 120 degrees. The crews wore helmets, and masks of chain mail to protect them from pieces of metal and rivets knocked loose from shells hitting the external armor."

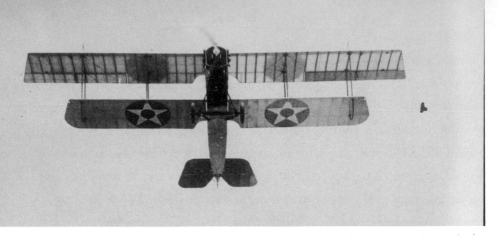

An American airplane is caught at the moment when its pilot is doing a loop in the air. This photograph shows how fragile early airplanes were. Yet Allied pilots were not allowed to use parachutes.

The British used tanks first, in 1916 at the Battle of the Somme. They started with forty-nine tanks. Seventeen broke down even before they got to the battlefield. Many of the ones left got stuck in muddy ground. "As we approached the Germans they let fire at us," wrote British Lieutenant Basil Henriques, who was in one of the tanks. "At first no damage was done and we retaliated, killing about 20. Then a smash . . . caused splinters to come in and the blood to pour down my face. Another minute and my driver got the same. . . . Then another smash, I think it must have been a bomb. . . . The next one wounded my driver so badly that we had to stop. By this time I could see nothing at all."

In the Battle of Cambrai in late 1917, tanks proved effective where the ground was firmer and the tank crews better trained. They managed to move five miles into German-held territory. "The English have brought in a new and terrible weapon," wrote German teenager Elfriede Kuhr. "These armoured vehicles are called tanks. No one is safe from them: they roll over every artillery battery, every trench, every position, and flatten them—not to mention what they do to the soldiers. Anyone who tries to take shelter in a shell-hole no longer has a chance." By 1918, the other Allies, including the Americans, were using tanks with success. The Germans never developed an effective tank of their own until after World War I, but they used captured British tanks to fight back.

World War I was the first war in which airplanes were used as weapons. The planes were relatively crude and hard to maneuver. At first they were used in place of hot-air balloons to observe the battlefield from above and report back on movements by the enemy. Airplane pilots not only had to observe field positions but also had to be on the lookout for enemy planes wanting to bring them down. Made of wood covered with canvas, the planes were easy to destroy. A plane would attempt to fly above an enemy plane and drop bricks to punch holes in its wings. Sometimes pilots used guns or grenades to bring the other plane down. The French were the first to fasten machine guns to airplanes.

Parachutes had been invented—soldiers in observation balloons wore them—but air pilots were not given them until 1918, and then only in Germany. Military leaders thought that having a parachute would make pilots more likely to bail out than engage in combat. The death rate among pilots was very high, for soon airplanes were not just used for spy missions. German and Allied pilots fought one-on-one with each other as well. These battles were called "dogfights," and they required great skill. Many of the pilots died. The ones who succeeded again and again became famous worldwide. Pilots who shot down five planes were called "aces." Perhaps the two most famous were Manfred von Richthofen—the German "Red Baron"—and the American Eddie Rickenbacker. "At 150 yards [from a German Pfalz plane] I pressed my triggers," Rickenbacker wrote of one fight. "The tracer bullets cut a streak of living fire into the rear of the Pfalz tail. . . . The swerving of its course indicated that its rudder no longer was held by a directing hand. At 2,000 feet above the enemy's lines I pulled up my headlong dive and watched the enemy machine continue on its course. . . . [T]he Pfalz circled a little to the south and the next minute crashed into the ground."

But by 1916, solo airplane flights and dogfights were less common. Planes flew in groups or squadrons. They dropped bombs on trenches and cut down troops with machine-gun fire from the air. They also bombed enemy cities. On June 13, 1917, fourteen German planes dropped more than one hundred bombs on London, killing 162 civilians, the highest number of deaths in London during the war. German airplanes also bombed Paris. In the spring of 1918, the British and French began bombing German cities. Their main objective was to knock out German industries, but they also frightened civilians in places like Frankfurt and Mannheim.

Submarines—or U-boats—played a major part in the war at sea. The Allies had submarines, but the German subs that went after Allied merchant

German submarines proved dangerous to Allied ships throughout the war. This photograph captures the moment when the crew of German *U-58* came out of their sub to surrender to the American destroyer USS *Fanning* on November 17, 1917. This was the first time in the war that an American ship captured a German vessel at sea.

ships were the most famous and saw the most action. They sank some 5,000 merchant ships during the war. The convoy system helped greatly to protect Allied ships after 1917, but there were still losses.

Submarines were almost impossible to spot when submerged. The British developed a "hydrophone"—an underwater microphone to pick up sounds—but it was still difficult to locate the subs exactly. By the end of 1918, 178 U-boats had been sunk by the Allies, but Germany was quick to replace them with new ones.

Submarine crews lived in very tight quarters. Johannes Speiss, a German officer on a U-boat, explained that the watch officer's "bunk was too small to permit him to lie on his back. He was forced to lie on one side and then, being wedged between the bulkhead to the right and the clothes-press on the left, to hold fast against the movements of the boat in a seaway." The center of the sub "served as a passageway . . . [where] a folding table could be inserted. Two folding camp-chairs completed the furniture. While the . . . [officers] took their meals, men had to pass back and forth through the boat, and each time anyone passed the table had to be folded." Inside the submarine was hotter than the sea, so drops of water formed on the steel structure. These drops fell onto the sleeping sailors. "Efforts were made to prevent this by covering the face with rain clothes or rubber sheets," said Speiss. "It was in reality like a damp cellar."

The countries that fought in World War I had a continual need for submarines and all the other ships, vehicles, and weapons necessary to fight. Many of these were made in Europe, but the United States, both before and after it became a combatant, remained a big provider. Producing weapons and food and encouraging civilian participation kept the American home front very busy during the war.

JAMES MONTGOMERY FLAGG.

TOGETHER WE WIN

UNITED STATES SHIPPING BOARD · EMERGENCY FLEET CORPORATION

5
THE WAR ON OUR HOME FRONT

After three years of uncertainty about America's role,
President Wilson wanted *all* Americans to agree that war with Germany
was the right choice. The president himself had long been against military
involvement; he won the presidency in 1916 as the person "who kept us out
of war." By April 1917, what had changed? The immediate reason was unrestricted German submarine warfare. But Wilson, when he called for war,
expressed idealistic thoughts about world peace and democracy. He couldn't
point to an attack on the United States to rally everyone. (Even the attack
on the *Lusitania*, which might have provoked war, had happened two years

A sailor, a workman, and a soldier join arms to show that all Americans—military and
civilian alike—needed to work together to win the war. This poster was designed by James
Montgomery Flagg, probably the most famous poster artist of the time. Hundreds of
posters were used as propaganda to encourage patriotic spirit and persuade Americans
to support the war effort.

earlier.) Instead, he talked about a moral vision. He needed to convince Americans that it was a moral duty to help do their part to end the war in Europe so that the United States could play an important role in bringing stability and justice to the world.

When the United States entered the war, American opinion was still divided. There were those who favored it—and felt we should have taken part earlier—but also those who opposed it—pacifists, progressives, various immigrant groups, and political opponents in Congress and state politics. How could Wilson achieve a united response in support of the war? One way was to educate people, even children, on the importance of the war.

World War I was a total war. This meant not only that the country would call out many men for the military but that every civilian would do his or her part for the war effort. The economy was based around training, feeding, clothing, transporting, and sustaining the armed forces. Food, uniforms, weapons, and raw materials like coal and steel were all in demand.

Even before the country entered the war, it had built up a war economy. The Allies needed the same goods and weapons the Americans would later need. From 1914 to 1918, the United States' income from trade went from a little less than $1.5 billion to a little more than $4 billion a year (from $27.7 billion to $74 billion in today's money). American businesses, factories, and farms were turning out guns, ammunition, wheat, copper, rubber, steel, gasoline, and the thousands of other products that kept the war going. In 1916, the federal government was spending about $477 million on American goods. Once the United States joined the Allies, the figure rose to $8.45 billion in 1918. The transition to a war economy in the United States was made easier because Americans had already expanded the necessary industries to supply the Allies.

Business was booming, and this meant more money for owners and plenty of jobs and higher salaries for workers. The unemployment rate dropped from

7.9 percent to 1.4 percent. Nearly every American who wanted to work was employed. An estimated 3 million people were in military service, and half a million workers joined the government. Adding other jobs like mining and manufacturing, about 44 million Americans were working in 1918. Two hundred thousand of those workers built airplanes, and at its peak, the aircraft industry turned out more than 12,000 airplanes a year.

But the United States was not producing airplanes designed by Americans. Automobile companies converted to make airplanes were turning out British training aircraft, fighter planes, and airplane engines. The U.S. government focused on manufacturing the British DH-4, the de Havilland. In fact, because the United States entered the war quickly and late—and because it was already producing equipment for the French and British—many American soldiers went into battle with British and French guns, gas masks, and other equipment. Nor could the United States keep up with producing enough ships to transport its soldiers to France. For all its output, the country failed to supply American troops with enough standardized American weapons: They were dependent on Allied gear.

There were both good and bad aspects to rapid mobilization—getting the country ready for war. For the first time, more women and African Americans had the opportunity to get better-paying and skilled jobs in factories and industries. But because of the shortage of men, who had become soldiers, children were also called upon to work. Child labor laws were overlooked as children took jobs in factories, bakeries, and grocery stores and on farms. A lot of newspapers were published during World War I, and the newspaper boy became a common figure on street corners. Teenagers also lied about their age so that they could join the army or navy.

The government called on both children and adults to help the war effort in several ways. Although there was no strict rationing in the United States—

except for a few months in 1918 when sugar was rationed—American civilians were encouraged to conserve food and fuel so that soldiers and sailors would not face shortages. (Sometimes, partly because of transportation problems, soldiers did anyway.) One card distributed to housewives urged them to "Go back to simple food. . . . Pray hard, work hard, sleep hard, and play hard. Do it all courageously and cheerfully." The government strongly suggested

Even before the United States entered World War I, American factories were producing a large number of weapons and products for the Allies. These women are working on the factory floor of a weapons plant in Massachusetts. The war called men away to be soldiers, and women often filled the gap. Some of them worked at skilled jobs like this that were previously not open to them.

wheatless days and meatless days. They placed ads in magazines: "Food is sacred. . . . Wheatless days in America make sleepless nights in Germany. . . . If U fast U beat U boats. . . . Serve beans by all means."

The making of "victory bread" was encouraged, using a substitute for wheat like corn, barley, rice, oats, rye flour, or potatoes. American wheat was feeding the American armed services, the Allied armies, and Allied civilians. One flyer asked American women to:

SAVE WHEAT
Will you help the Women of France?
They are struggling against starvation
and trying to feed not only themselves
and children: but their husbands and sons
who are fighting in the trenches

Children were told to eat everything they were served, vegetables included. They were encouraged to keep "A Little American's Promise":

At table I'll not leave a scrap
Of food upon my plate,
And I'll not eat between meals but
For supper time I'll wait.

"Victory gardens" were planted in backyards, school yards, and small city plots to grow food that civilians could eat, while big farms fed the soldiers and Allies. Even the White House had a victory garden. It also had sheep to trim the lawn so that gardeners could work elsewhere. The wool was sold to raise money for the war.

With men away, women took on farming. "It has been demonstrated that our girls from college and city trade can do farm work, and do it with a will," wrote Harriet Stanton Blatch in 1918. "And still better, at the end of the season their health wins high approval from the doctors and their work golden opinions from the farmers." These young women "ventured out on a new enterprise that meant aching muscles, sunburn and blisters, but not one . . . 'ever lost a day' in their eight hours at hard labor, beginning at four-thirty each morning for eight weeks during one of our hottest summers. They ploughed with horses, they ploughed with tractors, they sowed the seed, they thinned and weeded the plants, they reaped, they raked, they pitched the hay, they did fencing."

The U.S. government also asked that Americans conserve fuel. Coal was almost always in short supply. Civilians were asked to use firewood in its place. Children were given tags to tie to family coal shovels, giving information on how to save fuel. A coal shortage in 1918 closed "nonessential" businesses— those not connected with the war—during January, February, and March. From the fall of 1917 on, businesses were not allowed to use electricity to light signs at night. A "lightless night order" said they could be lit only from 7:45 to 11:00 p.m., and they had to be dark on Thursday and Sunday nights. In January 1918, Marie Tice wrote to her brother at the front, "Guess you have heard the latest on the coal situation. A legal holiday every Monday . . . and a complete industrial shutdown for five days beginning Saturday." Another relative wrote, "You should see good old New York by night, darkness on all sides—and every store closed."

The U.S. government did not pass laws to require civilians to follow these

These children display a giant head of cabbage grown in the "war garden" of Public School 88 in Queens, New York. Many Americans planted "war" or "victory" gardens near their homes and schools, growing their own food so that there would be no shortage for soldiers.

suggestions. It did establish government agencies to monitor aspects of the home front and to persuade civilians to follow their guidelines. These agencies included members of the government, business and industrial leaders, and other civilians. The four most important were the Food Administration (led by Herbert Hoover, who would serve as president of the United States from 1929 to 1933); the Fuel Administration; the Railroad Administration to coordinate transportation; and the War Industries Board, which tried to make manufacturing more efficient. It set up a priorities system for industries to fill the most essential orders from the U.S. government and Allies first. A priority system places the most important tasks at the top, with less important tasks coming later.

One of the biggest government programs promoted ways for civilians to help pay for the war. The Wilson administration did not want to raise taxes. (Eventually it had to.) Instead, it asked people to support Liberty loans. Americans could buy Liberty bonds—in effect, loaning the government the money they cost. They could then redeem them after the war for the amount they loaned, plus a bonus—known as interest. The first Liberty loan drive was set to raise $2 billion ($37 billion in today's money). "We went direct to the people, and that means to everybody—to business men, workmen, farmers, bankers, millionaires, school-teachers, laborers," said William McAdoo, Secretary of the Treasury. "We capitalized [on] the profound impulse called patriotism. It is the quality . . . that holds a nation together; it is one of the deepest and most powerful of human motives." Even children contributed their own money to buy bonds, or, more usually, the cheaper War Savings Stamps.

McAdoo traveled throughout the country, encouraging people to buy Liberty bonds. Movie stars like Mary Pickford and Douglas Fairbanks spoke to huge crowds. The government was happy to have the Boy Scouts encourage the buying of bonds. "[E]very Scout [has] a wonderful opportunity to do his share for his country under the slogan 'Every Scout To Save a Soldier,'" wrote President Wilson to the Boy Scouts' president. Bond drive posters by famous artists were put up everywhere.

"There was a wonderful Liberty Loan Parade on Friday," wrote one New Yorker in April 1918. "We got the PM off and stood from 2:30 till 6:30 watching it. . . . In school I sold 51 bonds amounting to $4800. We had a rally on . . . Sat. night and you never heard such thrilling talks as those children gave. . . . One clever stunt . . . for getting bonds [sold] by original ways was performed by a man . . . [who] climbed up to the Fire escape and rapped on the window for people to come out and buy bonds. They came & then he continued his climb until he had everyone out on the fire-escapes and a few hundred on the street. He sold quite a few bonds."

There were five loan campaigns, each set to raise a certain amount of money. Americans were not just asked to give; they were pressured to give. "A man who can't lend his government $1.25 [$19.70 in 2015] a week at the rate of 4% interest is not entitled to be an American citizen," declared McAdoo in one speech in California. But not everyone agreed. Tom W. Black and several other firefighters in Spokane, Washington, felt they had to resign from the fire department rather than buy bonds, because of their religious beliefs as members of the International Bible Students' Association (later the Jehovah's Witnesses). "I have been in the department for eight years," said Black, "and have a wife and four children. I am sorry that circumstances have arisen that compel me to resign to maintain my freedom of conscience, but I guess it can not be helped."

Liberty loans were not enough to finance the war. By May 1918, the government's debt was increasing by about a million dollars ($15.7 million in today's money) each month. Despite strong opposition, especially from the wealthy, Congress eventually passed laws calling for higher taxes on income

and on business profits. These were lowered after the war ended but were never again as low as taxes were before the war began.

The government used another tool to arouse patriotic feelings: propaganda, information used to spread one point of view, whether it was accurate or biased. U.S. Commissioner of Education P. P. Claxton organized teachers and university professors to create "war study courses" for young people at every level. He did not want these courses to be overly patriotic, but he did want them to represent the government's point of view that war was necessary. The courses were written up in pamphlets distributed to teachers. One for elementary school teachers suggested that it was useful to stir up students' "imagination and . . . emotions" against Germany. The elementary school courses stressed "patriotism, heroism, and sacrifice," which their country asked even of its young citizens. The important message was that the United States was a democracy. Germany was "autocratic"—a country run by one man, Kaiser Wilhelm II. Germany had done terrible things to civilians in Belgium and France, killing and burning innocent people. Americans had "to keep the German soldiers from coming to our country and treating us the same way."

The course for high school students stressed that only Germany, not the Allies, had caused the war and that only the Allies really wanted peace. It added that a military, warlike culture dominated German society and its soldiers were immoral and cruel. It ignored the role of the Allies in keeping the war going and in wanting a total victory that would destroy Germany's military and take away its power. It also ignored the fact that Britain and France had huge colonial empires in Africa and Asia, which their armies helped them control. Since colonies were ruled by other, mostly European, countries and not the people living there, they went against President Wilson's stated desire for each country to have its own government by the people.

Oversimplifying the war —portraying it in black and white, with no room for complexity or doubt—was not confined to teaching materials. In April 1917, the government formed the Committee on Public Information (CPI), an agency to provide government-approved information and publicity about the war to newspapers, magazines, and the general public. George Creel headed the committee. He was a newspaper editor and an investigative journalist —someone who exposed corruption in government and business. But his job at the CPI was to promote the government's thinking. The committee had many sections—the best-known ones were the Division of Pictorial Publicity, the News Division, and the Four Minute Men Division. The Committee on Public Information was by far the most powerful and influential publicity and propaganda organization the United States government had ever had or the world had ever seen.

Creel created "the Four Minute Men," some 75,000 civilian volunteers who gave short speeches before the public. They spoke in any place they had an audience—movie theaters, churches, and labor union meetings among them. (Four minutes was the time it took to change film reels in movie the-aters.) They spoke in favor of the draft, rationing of food and raw materi-als, buying war bonds, and anything else that might support the war. By the end of the war, Creel claimed, the Four Minute Men had given 7.5 million speeches to more than 314 million Americans. There were Four Minute Men who gave their speeches in many languages, including Yiddish, Polish, Italian, Russian, and Bohemian-Slovak, and even a Sioux Indian who spoke to Native Americans.

The CPI supplied the speakers with tips on what they should say. A bulletin issued by the committee in May 1917 advised, "The speech must not be longer than four minutes, which means there is no time for a single wasted word. . . . There never was a speech yet that couldn't be improved. Never be satisfied with success. Aim to be more successful, and still more successful. So keep your eyes open. Read all the papers every day, to find a new slogan . . . or a new idea to replace something you have in your speech. For instance, the editorial page of the *Chicago Herald* of May 19 . . . says, 'No country was ever saved by the other fellow; it must be done by you, by a hundred million yous, or it will not be done at all.' . . . Try slogans like 'Earn the right to say I helped to win the war,' and . . . 'A cause that is worth living for is worth dying for, and a cause that is worth dying for is worth fighting for.'"

In the beginning of its work, the CPI wanted to persuade people to support the war. The committee's *Official Bulletin* did distribute many facts about how government agencies worked. During the course of the war, it sent out 6,000 press releases and 75 million copies of more than thirty pamphlets. But as the war continued, more of its materials were straightforward propaganda. It ran advertisements in major magazines, encouraging ordinary Americans to report anyone who was negative about the war or spoke too loudly for peace. The Four Minute Men were advised they could speak about "horrible" crimes that the Germans had committed—though the huge majority of these rumors were false, including the intentional killing of babies.

Films produced by the CPI became more and more viciously anti-German, like *The Kaiser: The Beast of Berlin*, which portrayed the German leader as aggressive, greedy, and immoral. Increasing pressure was put on American media to publicize the committee's efforts. Toward the end of 1918, the CPI produced *Under Four Flags*—British, French, American, and Italian—"THE authentic record of actual fighting on the famous battle fronts of Europe."

A letter to movie theater managers stressed that the film was "a picture that the Government intends every one in the United States shall see . . . as an example of what the United States and the Allies . . . are doing for the cause of Liberty. . . . You owe it to your Government and to every American citizen in your neighborhood to show 'UNDER FOUR FLAGS' in your theatre. . . . It will increase their belief that you are a good business man as well as a patriotic citizen."

The CPI did not have legal authority to censor any newspaper or magazine, but it gave out "voluntary guidelines" that it expected would be followed. In order to keep their connections with government and military sources and learn up-to-the-minute news, most journalists followed them. Laws passed by Congress, however, directly permitted censorship. Wilson had said in his request for Congress to declare war, "If there should be any disloyalty, it will be dealt with with a firm hand of stern repression." Now the government would decide what "disloyalty" would be. Not every member of Congress agreed with censorship. As a law called "the Espionage Act" was being debated, it "has all the earmarks of a dictatorship," said Republican Senator William E. Borah from Idaho. "It suppresses free speech and does it all in the name of war and patriotism."

But the Espionage Act was passed and became law in 1917. It stated, "Every letter, writing, circular, postal card, picture, print, engraving, photograph, newspaper, pamphlet, book, or other publication . . . of any kind, containing any matter advocating or urging treason, insurrection, or forcible resistance to any law of the United States, is hereby declared to be nonmailable." Under it, the government could prevent anything printed from being sent through the mail. If magazines, journals, or newspapers could not be mailed, they could not reach their readers.

This was a strong form of censorship: one written piece declared disloyal could prevent thousands of people from reading it. Postmaster General Albert Burleson used this power to censor the writings of pacifists, socialists, and other political radicals if he decided they opposed the federal government. Although "espionage" usually means spying, in 1917 the act, as Senator Borah understood, was aimed at limiting free speech. It allowed the government to fine and/or imprison anyone who said something it considered untrue that was meant to "interfere with the operation or success of the military or naval forces." This included anyone who spoke out against the draft or tried to encourage men not to join the military services.

Eugene Debs (right) and Victor Berger (left) were both arrested under the Espionage Act and the Sedition Act. Debs went to jail for giving a speech that blamed the war on business interests. Berger was also sentenced to prison for publishing a socialist newspaper, but he appealed his sentence and was never jailed. Bertha Hale White, the woman between them, was a journalist and teacher who also worked for the American Socialist Party.

The charge of "unpatriotic" became used as a weapon against even mild opposition. "I . . . planned an *Anti-Enlistment League*, which should line up all men and women who should promise never to enlist voluntarily or to give approval to such enlistment on the part of others," remembered Jessie Wallace Hughan. "As I was a high school teacher at this time, and still am, the league, which received more publicity than its importance deserved, was the subject of much hostile comment in the Brooklyn papers. I was an active Socialist, also, and always talked against the war in speeches that I made. This activity caused me to be examined before superintendents and boards of examiners several times, the general surveillance and excitement lasting through the war and after."

In 1918, Congress passed the Sedition Act. "Sedition" means acting or speaking to encourage people to rebel against a government. The Sedition Act expanded the Espionage Act. It gave greater power to the U.S. government to arrest anyone accused of antiwar or antimilitary actions. It could be used to punish anyone who said or published "any disloyal, profane, scurrilous or abusive language about the form or government of the United States, or the Constitution." Again, this included antidraft speech or action as a punishable offense. Under the Sedition Act, the government could arrest anyone who spoke out against lending money to the Allies or buying Liberty bonds to support the war.

There was reason to protect war industries and the military from violent actions. There had already been some acts of espionage even before the United States entered the war. Germans and Americans sympathetic to Germany had blown up a factory making weapons in New Jersey in July 1916. But it was one thing to arrest someone for a disloyal action; it was another to arrest them for a thought. Under the Espionage and Sedition Acts, a person could go to jail for what he wrote or spoke. Eugene Debs was one of these. Five times a Socialist candidate for president of the United States, he was sentenced to ten years in jail for giving a speech that blamed the war on business interests. "[T]he working class who fight all the battles, . . . who make the supreme sacrifices, . . . who freely shed their blood . . . have never yet had a voice in either declaring war or making peace," said Debs. "It is the ruling class that . . . does both." Debs's sentence was commuted in 1921.

Victor Berger was the first Socialist congressman to be elected in the United States. As the editor of the *Milwaukee Leader*, he spoke out against the war. Postmaster General Burleson charged him three times with breaking the Espionage Act. He could no longer mail his newspaper to its readers. In 1919, he was sentenced to twenty years in jail, but he appealed his conviction. The Supreme Court ruled in his favor in 1921, and he was reelected to Congress.

Berger was an immigrant from Austria-Hungary. Immigrants received particular attention from the government and from the American people during the war. By 1917, there were huge numbers of immigrants living in the United States. Many who had come since 1870 were Italian, eastern European, or Jewish. They often continued to speak their native languages. They often lived in poverty. Even before World War I they seemed foreign and threatening to many Americans, who did not believe they could ever fit into mainstream society in the United States. The war heightened those fears. Were immigrants loyal to the United States or to their home countries? Most Americans wanted a united country in time of war—one in which people put aside their ethnic loyalties and foreign customs to be unquestionably patriotic. This was the root of the "100 percent American" campaign, supported by the CPI and many public organizations, to quickly teach immigrants English, educate them about American values, and turn them into citizens.

Progressive social workers and others had been trying for several years to "Americanize" immigrants and their children to give them better opportunities for jobs, education, and fitting into American society. But when the United States entered the war, this became an urgent pressure. The CPI created a Division of Work with the Foreign-Born. It formed Loyalty Leagues among different ethnic groups, distributing patriotic propaganda to them in their own languages. On July 4, 1918, the CPI brought men and women from thirty-three ethnic groups to respectfully walk by President George Washington's tomb at his home in Mount Vernon, Virginia—what today might be called "a photo opportunity." While events like this one were positive and cheerful, there was another side to the CPI's work with immigrants. The committee used people fluent in immigrant languages, many of them college professors, to read foreign-language newspapers and other publications. They reported back to the CPI on any "material which may fall under the Espionage Act." Although the CPI could not censor them, they could pass this information back to people like Postmaster General Burleson, who did.

Actually, the vast majority of immigrants showed their patriotism in many ways. They bought Liberty bonds. Half a million foreign-born soldiers served in the U.S. armed forces—18 percent of all soldiers and sailors. Immigrants also held jobs in many war-related industries, including mining, lumber, and the production of iron and steel. In the workplace, however, they encountered another kind of prejudice and fear if they supported unions or workers' rights. Many Americans believed that socialists and anarchists (people who believed there should be no governments or laws) stirred up trouble and discontent among workers. They believed that Italian and Russian immi-

German immigrants were made to register as enemy aliens with the U.S. Justice Department. This is a page from the registration form of Hans Joachim von Fischer-Treuenfeld, who lived in Kansas City, Kansas. His story seems unusual. After Germany declared war, he reported to the German consul in New Orleans to serve as a reservist in the German army, but was dismissed. He later asked to be detained because he was being badly treated by Americans, who thought he was a German spy.

3

15. Have you since January 1, 1914, reported to or registered with a consul or representative of any country other than the United States for military or naval or other service? *Yes.* (Answer "Yes" or "No.") If yes, state when and where and to whom and for what country and for what service *at outbreak of this war I reported as Reservist et to the German General consuls at New-Orleans, but was dismissed as there was no transportation. My last communication with the Germany!*

16. Have you ever been arrested or detained on any charge? *Yes* (Answer "Yes" or "No.") If yes, state when, where, and on what charges? *Abusing the person of the German consular agent* on parole? *Charge dismissed by Court* at *Kansas-City M?* (Answer "Yes 1917 City Hall K.C. M?"

17. Have you a permit to enter forbidden areas? *yes* (Answer "Yes" or "No.") If yes, state number of permit *F 7861*

I solemnly swear that all the above statements and answers by me made are true.

(Signature) *Hansjoachim von Fischer-Treuenfeld?*

Sworn to before me this *8th February* 19*18*

at *Police Headquarters Kansas City Kans*

Wos Thomas (Registration officer)

Secretary Police Dept (Official title, police or post office.)

Left thumb print, if registrant can not write.

DESCRIPTION OF REGISTRANT.
(To be filled in by registration officer.)

Hansjoachim von Fischer-Treuenfeld

Age *27* years. Mouth *Small*
Height 5 ft. *6* in. Chin *Square*
Weight *134* Hair *Light Brown*
Forehead *High* Complexion *Light*
Eyes *Blue* Face *Oval*
Nose *Large*
Distinctive marks *Ears Prominent ear right cheek light mustache*
Name *Hansjoachim von Fischer-Treuenfeld*
Address *714 Barnett Ave. Kansas City Kans.*

89

These members of the Industrial Workers of the World (IWW) were held for eighteen months at Ellis Island because of their radical support for better conditions for laborers. They are shown here in 1919, when they were released. The U.S. government detained thousands of antiwar advocates, socialists, and labor leaders, most of them immigrants who were not citizens. More than eight hundred people were deported back to their home countries.

grants, especially, brought radical ideas about laborers to the United States. In wartime the U.S. government and owners of business and industry both wanted production to run smoothly. Strikes and unions could interrupt the war effort. Therefore, the government had a stake in preventing workers from using the war to gain better pay or working conditions at the cost of decreased production. Employers could and did ignore the call for workers' rights by labeling such demands socialist or unpatriotic.

The American Federation of Labor (AFL), the largest union in the United States, had gone on record in support of war just before it was declared. "It is our earnest hope that our republic may be safeguarded in its unswerving desire for peace," pledged the union on March 24, 1917. "But despite all our endeavors and hopes, should our country be drawn into the maelstrom of the European conflict, we, with these ideals of liberty and justice herein declared, as the indispensable basis for national policies, offer our services to our country in every field of activity to defend, safeguard and preserve the republic of the United States of America against its enemies . . . and we call upon our fellow workers and fellow citizens in the holy name of labor, justice, freedom and humanity to devotedly and patriotically give like service."

The wartime president of the AFL, Samuel Gompers, a British immigrant, did not believe that socialism was the way to better worker conditions. He envisioned a partnership of workers, employers, and government in which patience and fairness would prevail. In contrast, the Industrial Workers of the World (IWW), a smaller and far more radical union nicknamed the Wobblies, denounced business, industry, and the military for pushing the United States into war. The federal government tapped the union's phones and read its mail. Yet the IWW continued to agitate for the rights of working men and women through the war years. Between 1914 and 1920 there were more than 3,000 strikes a year; between 1916 and 1918 alone, more than 4 million workers went on strike.

Some employers used violence to break the strikes. They used privately hired security men, and sometimes regular police or federal troops, to attack strikers. They evicted families who lived in company-owned homes. When copper miners struck in Bisbee, Arizona, in June 1917, city law enforcers forced hundreds of strikers onto trains, then left them in the desert without food or water. In Butte, Montana, IWW organizer Frank Little, also working with copper miners, was dragged from his house and lynched. Lynching is the mob murder of someone believed to have committed a crime or violated social customs. A mob does not follow the rule of the law. Though government leaders and newspapers objected to lynching, the *New York Times* wrote that "the IWW agitators are in effect, and perhaps in fact, agents of Germany. The Federal authorities should make short work of these treasonable conspirators against the United States."

After 1917, everything German came under attack. German Americans, even longtime citizens, experienced severe discrimination—and outright hatred—because they came from the country of America's enemy. Perhaps many Americans did not realize that German Americans also served in the armed forces. "Two sons, Charlie and August went to the World War," said Judge J. Faudie, an immigrant from Germany. "August was in France, and was in the army of occupation after the war closed. . . . I have become an American citizen long ago, and was glad that my boys could serve this country of my adoption . . . even if we were not here in those early days."

Although the German language had been taught in schools throughout the country, almost half of the states eliminated it from classes. Orchestras stopped playing music by German composers like Ludwig van Beethoven. "It is still a question in my mind whether it is for the good of the country to abolish a treasure of art which does not belong to Germany but to the world," famous conductor Leopold Stokowski wrote to President Wilson. "If, in your opinion, it is necessary for the good of the nation that the music of Bach and Beethoven be abolished from our concert programs, it is needless to say that I shall unquestionably abide by your decision." Wilson suggested Stokowski listen to the public, which at this time was against almost everything German.

German-origin expressions changed—sauerkraut became "liberty cabbage" and hamburger "liberty sandwich." German measles were called "liberty measles." "Those who opposed or did not readily accept the United States' entry into the War (especially, of course, if they happened to be of German ancestry) were labeled 'pro-Germans,'" remembered A. J. Muste, a Protestant minister. "People began to act as amateur spies and loyalty agents, reporting mysterious circles of light in the windows of neighbors living somewhere near the shore, which were assumed to be signals to prowling German submarines." Robert Prager, a German immigrant in Collinsville, Illinois (who had tried to enlist in the navy), was accused of attempting to blow up a mine and lynched.

But perhaps the most anger and contempt went toward conscientious objectors (COs)—those who refused to fight because of religious or personal beliefs. Some agreed to work for the army or the country in jobs where they did not have to carry weapons or kill. These included farming on the home front and aiding the wounded in France. But some COs refused even alternative service. Roger Baldwin, a social worker and pacifist, stated in a court hearing about whether he should be jailed: "I am not seeking to evade the draft. . . . I scorn evasion, compromise and gambling with moral issues. It may . . . be argued that the War Department's liberal provision for agricultural service . . . for conscientious objectors would be open to me if I obey the law . . . and that there can be no moral objection to farming . . . I can make no moral distinction between the various services which assist in prosecuting a war—whether rendered in the trenches, in the purchase of bonds or thrift stamps at home, or in raising farm products under the lash of the draft act. All serve the same end—war." Baldwin served nine months in jail for refusing to register for the draft. He became one of the founders of the American Civil Liberties Union, which continues today to give legal help to citizens fighting for their civil rights.

COs who did agree to serve as noncombatants in the army were often harassed by other soldiers and officers. Erling H. Lunde was "punished for not doing 'camp police,' namely cutting grass on the post, by being put in solitary confinement on bread and water for three days."

Conscientious objectors were often considered "slackers." During World War I this meant anyone who avoided military service. The word "slackers" conveyed laziness and even cowardice. It was used to insult young men who were not in the armed forces and was sometimes directed even toward those who had tried to enlist but were rejected for medical reasons. An enthusiastic "patriot" might not bother to find the reason why a man was not in military uniform. One did not have to be a CO or a labor organizer or a socialist publisher or an immigrant to be charged with disloyalty. With emotions running high in wartime, and a federal government determined to establish unity of thought, anyone might find himself or herself accused of not being 100 percent American.

The federal government grew larger and more powerful during World War I. This was not particularly what Wilson or the Americans who served in his government and on the war boards wanted. They believed they could persuade—and sometimes harass—civilians into doing what was needed to fight the war. But World War I demanded more of government and citizens than any war before it. It took an increased income tax to fund it—even though tax rates might go down afterward, they would never be as low as they were before the First World War. By creating committees to oversee production and conservation, government showed Americans that it could be useful in helping to run the country in a crisis and reach out to citizens at every level. This was something progressives and socialists had hoped for. But the war also demonstrated that the U.S. government could use propaganda on a large scale to win the loyalty of Americans and censor those who disagreed.

One way Americans showed their support of the war on the home front was to raise money. These Red Cross volunteers, including Boy Scouts, collected contributions during a parade in Birmingham, Alabama.

"Liberty And Freedom Shall Not Perish"
A. Lincoln

COLORED MEN
The First Americans
Who Planted
Our Flag
on the
Firing Line

CHAS. GUSTRINE CHICAGO

TRUE SONS OF FREEDOM

6

AFRICAN AMERICANS AT WAR AND AT HOME

At the end of April 1917, three weeks after the United States had declared war on Germany, a letter signed by "a Negro Educator" circulated through the small town of Friars Point, Mississippi. "Young negro men and boys what have we to fight for in this country?" it asked. "Nothing. Some of our well educated negroes are touring the country urging our young race to be killed up like sheep, for nothing. If we fight in this war time we fight for nothing. . . . [F]ight not for we will only be a . . . shield for the white race. After war we get nothing."

African Americans in 1917 had few civil rights and were denied opportunities for education, decent housing, and jobs. Even if they did not live under

This 1918 poster celebrates contributions by African Americans to wars fought by the United States. It shows black doughboys attacking Germans, with President Abraham Lincoln in the upper right, to remind viewers of how black soldiers served valiantly during the Civil War.

segregation in the South—where, for example, they could not eat in "whites only" restaurants and had to sit at the back of streetcars—they suffered from discrimination. They were prevented from voting and often faced racial violence in riots and lynchings.

African Americans had every reason to question why blacks should fight to defend democracy in Europe when they lived as second-class citizens in the United States. But when war was declared, many volunteered to serve in the U.S. Army. At first, "Negro enlistment was discouraged," wrote Emmett J. Scott, an African American and special assistant to the Secretary of War. The army, which had only a small number of black troops serving at the time, did not want more. Southern politicians expressed racist concerns if black men were drafted. That would result in "arrogant strutting representatives of the black soldiery in every community," said Mississippi Senator James K. Vardaman. However, America's military needed the manpower. Army leadership soon changed its mind. African Americans were drafted in large numbers, sometimes more than white men from the same towns and cities. White men were more likely to be exempted from service than black men. More than black men, white men had the kinds of skilled jobs in industry that allowed them exemptions. An estimated 370,000 African Americans served during World War I. They counted for 13 percent of the American military, while black people made up only about 10 percent of the U.S. population.

The majority of black Americans agreed with civil rights leader and editor W. E. B. Du Bois, who wrote, "Let us not hesitate. Let us, while this war lasts, forget our special grievances and close our ranks shoulder to shoulder with our white fellow citizens. . . . We make no ordinary sacrifice, but we make it gladly and willingly with our eyes lifted to the hills." Leaders like Du Bois believed that by showing loyalty and patriotism, fighting in the war would put them in a better position to gain civil rights at home when it was over. Ellen

This African American man, in his doughboy uniform, served in the AEF in France. Even though the federal government did not want to recruit black soldiers when the war started, it finally drafted more than 300,000 men.

Horace Pippin served in the 369th Infantry, the famous black combat unit. These pages from the autobiography he wrote and illustrated after the war shows three soldiers marching. Although Pippin's right hand was permanently injured, he became an extraordinary painter. Some of his work vividly portrays the African American experience of slavery and segregation.

Tarry of Alabama remembered supporting the war, but "though we carried huge signs in . . . a parade about fighting for democracy and how everybody should try to buy bonds, the Negro children were still put at the end of the procession." Charles Brodnax, a black farmer from Virginia, simply "felt that I belonged to the Government of my country and should answer to the call and obey the orders in defense of Democracy."

Having volunteered or been drafted, a black soldier had few opportunities for advancement in the U.S. military. He served in segregated units, almost always under white officers. (There was one segregated training camp for a small number of black officers in Iowa, but none could rise above the rank of captain.) Many of the military training camps for black, as well as white, men were in the South. White Americans feared that letting black Americans use guns would increase their pride and literally put a weapon into their hands.

On August 23, 1917, black troops from a "colored" battalion—not draftees, but all experienced soldiers—attacked white civilians in Houston, Texas. The soldiers had finally found the segregation laws intolerable. They killed seventeen people. The battalion was put under arrest, more than one hundred of the men were court-martialed, and more than a dozen were executed. This incident actually halted the draft of African Americans until September 22, while the army worked out a way to train black troops quickly in camps close to their homes—in hopes of avoiding further conflict—and then send them to France. Another reason the U.S. Army sped up the process, even if the troops were undertrained, was because more manpower was needed. (Many white troops also received little training before they were shipped to France.)

Perhaps because of the fear of arming them, only 20 percent of black soldiers served in combat units. The vast majority were placed in labor battalions. They unloaded ships, built roads, dug trenches, constructed buildings, salvaged weapons and equipment, and performed other physically demanding jobs. It was similar to work they did in the United States and disappointed many black leaders, who had hoped the war would prove the fighting abilities and courage of black soldiers.

Horace Pippin, who later became a well-known and respected artist, wrote an autobiography of his experiences in World War I. "I remember the day very well, that we left the good old USA," he wrote. "She was in trouble with Germany, and to do our duty . . . we had to go . . . and we did on the 17th of November 1917." In France Pippin and his unit "laid about five hundred miles of rail . . . and we went to bed in the dark and got out in the dark, only the moon shone and did give us a little light. . . . We were in water up to our knees all the time. It was slow work and wet work, you would go to bed wet."

Pippin did his share of labor, but he also served in combat with the 369th Infantry. The U.S. Army formed two black combat divisions, the 92nd and the 93rd. The 92nd Division was made up of men from several training camps who had not previously worked together. Training together made them more likely to know and understand what each one should do in battle. It also built up trust and comradeship between the officers and the soldiers. The 92nd Division did not do well in its first battles, but at the end of the war, through greater experience, its record improved. The 93rd Division, assembled from National Guardsmen (who already had training) and draftees from South Carolina, had an excellent record. They fought at the Meuse-Argonne and the Oise-Aisne in the summer and fall of 1918.

"I remember the first night that I put foot in No Man's Land," Pippin wrote. "It was the first time my company ever had any men in No Man's Land." He went on a scouting trip, creeping through wire into a shell hole. When he got back to his trench, "it was . . . raining, the water was dripping off of us. . . . We did not dare make a fire not even strike a match in the trench so it was not the first time I went to bed wet."

Pippin fought in the Argonne Forest several times. At one point, the Germans "gave us shell fire, and the gas was thick, and the forest looked as if it were ready to give up all of its trees every time a shell came crashing through. . . . There was a big acorn tree that stood by my dugout, it was a fine one. But . . . the shell tore off the top of it. We hardly knew what to do, for we could not fight shells. But we could [fight] the Germans. We would rather for the Germans to come over the top than to have their shells." Pippin was eventually shot and lost some of the use of his right arm, but it didn't later stop him from painting.

Four of the 93rd's regiments fought directly under French command.

Here African American infantry troops are marching near Verdun, France. This photograph was taken on November 5, 1918, one week before the armistice.

General Pershing advised the French officers commanding these black troops that they "must not eat with them, must not shake hands with them, seek to talk to them or to meet with them outside the requirements of military service. We must not commend too highly these troops, especially in front of white Americans."

Despite Pershing's racist suggestions, the 93rd Division thrived. The most famous of its units was the 369th Infantry, the one in which Pippin served.

Soldiers in the unit were called "the Harlem Hellfighters" because they came from the neighborhood of Harlem in New York City. These men spent 191 days at the front, longer than any other American regiment. As they marched toward the trenches for the first time, one black soldier remembered, "There were a whole lot of blind men, and one-legged men, and one-armed men, and sick men, all coming this way. I asked a white man where all these wounded men come from? And he says, 'N_____r, they're coming from right where you're going the day after tomorrow.'"

The 369th arrived at Minacourt, France. Their white commander, Major Warner Ross, described the scene: "Stones, dirt, shrapnel, limbs and whole trees filled the air. The noise and concussion alone were enough to kill you. Flashes of fire, the metallic crack of high explosives, the awful explosions that dug holes fifteen and twenty feet in diameter. The utter and complete pandemonium and the stench of hell, your friends blown to bits, the pieces dropping near you."

On May 15, 1918, two African Americans were on duty in the Argonne Forest. "While on night sentry duty, . . . [Pvt. Henry] Johnson and a fellow Soldier, Pvt. Needham Roberts, received a surprise attack by a German raiding party consisting of at least 12 soldiers," stated an official U.S. government citation for bravery years later.

"While under intense enemy fire and despite receiving significant wounds, Johnson mounted a brave retaliation resulting in several enemy casualties. When his fellow Soldier was badly wounded, Johnson prevented him from being taken prisoner by German forces.

"Johnson exposed himself to grave danger by advancing from his position to engage an enemy soldier in hand-to-hand combat. Wielding only a knife and being seriously wounded, Johnson continued fighting, took his Bolo knife and stabbed it through an enemy soldier's head.

"Displaying great courage, Johnson held back the enemy force until they retreated."

These two African American soldiers received the French Croix de Guerre (Cross of War). By the end of the war, the entire 369th Infantry and two other black regiments were honored by the French with the Croix de Guerre for courage under fire. Pershing reversed himself after the war, stating, "I cannot commend too highly the spirit shown among the colored combat troops, who exhibit fine capacity for quick training and eagerness for the most dangerous work." As for a reward from the United States, Henry Johnson, who died in 1929, received the Distinguished Service Cross posthumously (that is, after his death) in 2002. He finally received the United States' highest honor, the Medal of Honor, in 2015.

Despite blatant discrimination, black Americans admirably served their country. Melville Miller, who was sixteen when he joined the army, recalled a march through parts of France that had once been held by the Germans. "That day, the sun was shining. . . . And the band was playing," Miller said. "Everybody's head [was] high, and we were all proud to be Americans, proud to be black, and proud to be in the 15th New York Infantry."

At the same time African Americans were serving in France, those at home were going through major changes. After the economic recession of 1913, the war that started in Europe in 1914 created a demand for weapons, chemicals, metal products, and other materials needed by the Allies. But the war also diminished the wave of European immigrants who had been employed in large numbers in American factory and construction, as well as unskilled, work. Industries in the North had jobs to fill. Southern black Americans, tired of strict segregation and poverty, began to travel north and west to take advantage of the need for labor. "There is no advancement here for me," decided an African American living in Texas in 1917. "I would like

This porter, shown in 1917 with her supplies, cleaned the New York City subways. Although the majority of black people lived in the South, by 1914 many were heading north for jobs. Between 1914 and 1920, an estimated half a million African Americans moved to cities like New York, Chicago, and Detroit. This is known as "the Great Migration."

to come where I can better my condition[.] I want work and am not afraid to work. All I wish is a chance to make good."

"Because Negroes have made few public complaints about their condition in the South, the average white man has assumed that they are satisfied," wrote African American W. T. B. Williams in a government report; "but there is a vast amount of dissatisfaction among them over their lot. . . . [T]he Negro's list of grievances that have prepared him for this migration is a long one."

Between 1914 and 1920, some half a million African Americans left the South, moving to cities including New York, Chicago, Detroit, Pittsburgh, and Omaha. This was the beginning of what came to be known as "the Great Migration."

This migration of blacks created opportunities for them but also considerable racial tension. They faced discrimination in housing, education, and the job market. They tended to live in informally segregated neighborhoods, in poor housing, some "that had no water and no toilets, whose roofs leaked and whose cellars were flooded," reported one account in southeastern Pennsylvania. "Negroes were coming in a great dark tide from the South, and they had to have some place to live," remembered poet Langston Hughes. "Sheds and garages and store fronts were turned into living quarters. As always, the white neighborhoods resented Negroes moving closer and closer. . . ."

Black workers were also called upon to work as strikebreakers, crossing picket lines to take the jobs of strikers. They did this because they were often desperate for work and not allowed into unions. But this angered white laborers. There were race riots, with whites attacking black people, including one in East St. Louis on July 7, 1917. Forty-seven people died, among them thirty-nine African Americans. Lynchings continued, especially in southern states, which were anxious about losing so much black labor. Eighty blacks were lynched in 1915, fifty-four in 1916, thirty-eight in 1917, and fifty-eight in

1918. President Wilson himself said that "lynching is unpatriotic," but he also said that "the Federal Government has absolutely no jurisdiction over matters of this kind." On top of everything else, the Wilson administration began to segregate employees in federal jobs, which were not segregated in the late nineteenth or early twentieth centuries. Some federal services were also segregated. Black people who wanted to mail letters now had to go to segregated windows in post offices, both in the South and the North.

Did African Americans do better in the United States because of the war? "Optimism as to the status of the Negro after the war is ill-timed,"

Soldiers of the 369th Infantry, an African American combat regiment, arrive back in New York after their distinguished service in France. Known as "the Harlem Hellfighters"—Harlem is a traditionally black neighborhood in New York City—they were cheered by hundreds of thousands of black and white supporters in a victory parade on February 17, 1919.

wrote Chandler Owen, a black socialist, in March 1919. "Like all other people who have fought battles for their country, the Negro will have to return to engage in a political and industrial fight with his own country to secure his just rights. Not an inch or ell will be yielded except through compulsion and necessity. No one will say to the Negro, 'you have fought so gallantly and vigorously, your loyalty was so unadulterated and true, you were so patriotic that we are going to give you the vote in the South . . . segregation in places of public accommodation will be made unlawful; lynching will be stopped by the stern arm of Government.' . . . This indeed will not happen."

Owen was right, it did not even begin to happen, at least not until the desegregation of the military in 1948 and the civil rights movement of the 1950s and 1960s. In some ways, the situation was worse. As white men returned to civilian life, blacks lost their jobs. In 1919, several race riots broke out, in cities such as Chicago, Washington, Omaha, Charleston, and Knoxville. African Americans, including veterans of the war, continued to be lynched. But many blacks now lived permanently in the North, where, although they experienced discrimination, they were able to vote because there were no segregation laws or difficult registration tests to stop them, and they had a better chance of a good education. Organizations like the National Urban League, founded in 1910, helped them adapt to cities by finding them jobs and campaigning to open labor unions to African Americans. The National Association for the Advancement of Colored People (NAACP), founded in 1909, actively campaigned for black civil rights and would, in the 1930s, start a series of lawsuits against segregated education in the South. Gaining equality was a gradual process, and World War I did nothing major to advance it.

But the experience of being in France personally changed many African American soldiers even if it didn't change the attitudes of white people. Bill

Broonzy, a blues composer and singer, came home to Arkansas after serving in the war. "I had a nice uniform," he commented. "I met a white fellow that was knowin' me before I went into the army. So he told me, said, 'Listen, boy,' says, 'Now you been to the army.' I told him, 'Yeah.' He says, 'How'd you like it?' I said, 'It's OK.' He says, 'Well,' he says, 'you ain't in the army now. . . . And those clothes you got there . . . you can take 'em home an' get out of 'em an' get you some overhalls [overalls]. . . . Because there's no n_____r gonna walk around here with no Uncle Sam's uniform on up and down the streets here.'"

Racist comments like that didn't change the fact that black Americans had been treated well in France. "You know now that the mean, contemptible spirit of race prejudice that curses this land is not the spirit of other lands," Reverend Francis J. Grimké said to black soldiers returning from Europe in 1919. "[Y]ou know now what it is to be treated as a man . . . to be treated like real American men."

W. E. B. Du Bois summed it all up:

"We *return*.

"We *return from fighting*.

"We *return fighting*.

"Make way for Democracy! We saved it in France, and . . . we will save it in the United States of America, or know the reason why."

These children wave American flags as the soldiers of the 369th Infantry—who were honored by the French with medals for their bravery—march up Fifth Avenue in New York. Schools in Harlem declared a holiday on February 17, 1919, so that students could attend the victory parade.

7

WOMEN, SUFFRAGE, AND SERVICE

Women played a major part in the peace movement before
the United States entered World War I. They also supported preparedness.
But one of the biggest concerns for women just before and during the war
years was women's suffrage—the right to vote. When the war started, only
women in a few states could vote; most women could not. They had to decide whether to put aside the suffrage fight until the war was over or to keep
hammering at President Wilson and Congress to give them the vote.

Most women supported the decision to go to war. Anna Howard Shaw,
president of the National American Women's Suffrage Association, called on
each woman to "inspire, encourage and urge the men of her family to perform

Women have traditionally knitted garments, including socks, to keep soldiers warm
during wartime. In World War I, women knitted and rolled bandages, but they also
welded machinery, drove trucks, served in combat areas as nurses, and worked as
telephone operators for the army in France.

their patriotic duty. This is the service of sacrifice and loyalty which the Government asks of the women of the nation at the present critical hour." Women believed that if they showed their patriotism and willingness to work for the war effort, it would persuade male members of Congress to grant them suffrage.

Congress was not ready to agree. Many of those who opposed the female vote believed that women were on the side of peace, that they thought as mothers did of protecting their sons, and that they were naive and emotional—that they would vote against politicians who supported defense and would make the United States weak. This had nothing to do with fact. Many women had supported preparedness. The suffragists themselves had split into two groups, one using traditional methods of persuasion, the other civil disobedience. The militant National Women's Party, founded by Alice Paul and Lucy Burns, picketed the White House, enduring threats and violence.

Even after the United States entered the war, they continued to picket the White House. Many Americans felt this was unpatriotic. The National Women's Party felt the issue of votes for women was just as important during war as during peace. The women held up banners that challenged, "How long must women wait for liberty?" They marched through the streets of cities. They sang protest songs, often with special lyrics set to older music, like this one, called "Rise Up Women!" set to the Civil War fighting song "John Brown's Body":

Rise up, women, for the fight is hard and long;
Rise up in thousands singing loud a battle song.
Right is might, and in strength we shall be strong
And the cause goes marching on
Glory, glory, hallelujah! Glory, glory, hallelujah!
Glory, glory, hallelujah! The cause goes marching on.

The women who picketed were brave and determined. They were physically attacked—sometimes banners were torn from their hands. Some of these read "Kaiser Wilson," a reference to the undemocratic leader of Germany that suggested that President Wilson was undemocratic for not giving women the vote. Over four days in June, twenty-nine women were arrested. Six were fined but refused to pay the fine and were sent to prison. Sixteen more women were arrested in

Women picket the White House on January 25, 1917, calling for the right to vote. After the United States entered the war, some suffragists stopped such actions of civil disobedience. Others continued to picket and go to jail because they believed the vote for women was part of the larger issue of guaranteeing freedom for all, which President Wilson stressed as a reason to go to war. The signs they carried used Wilson's own words about liberty.

July. The Espionage Act had already been passed, and the judge who tried these women considered charging them under it. But the only quotations written on their picket signs were from President Wilson's speeches about democracy. Instead, they were convicted for obstructing traffic. Wilson pardoned all the women.

In October, Alice Paul, Lucy Burns, and nine other women were arrested. One suffragette spoke out at her trial: "As long as women have to go to jail for petty offenses to secure freedom for the women of America, then we will continue to go to jail."

The women were sent to the Occoquan workhouse in northern Virginia, the prison used for people convicted of crimes in Washington, D.C. They considered themselves political prisoners, not criminals, and refused to work in the garden or sewing room, the work assigned to women prisoners. The head of the workhouse "announced . . . that there will be no visitors for the ladies and they will not be allowed to communicate with any one," reported the *Washington Post*. In mid-November 1917, sixteen women, led by Alice Paul, began hunger strikes. "Mrs. Lawrence Lewis . . . and Miss Lucy Burns . . . were removed from Occoquan to jail Tuesday, where they were forcibly fed, Miss Burns by means of a tube through the nose," stated the *Post*.

Because of this harsh treatment, more Americans began to agree that it was time for women's suffrage. New York State gave women the vote in November 1917. Wilson himself came to support votes for women, informing Congress in 1918 that women's suffrage "is vital to the winning of the war." He was talking not about the protesters but about all the women on the home front and in France whose work was contributing to the war effort. However, it took until 1919 for both the Senate and the House of Representatives to approve an amendment to the Constitution giving women the right to vote. After the needed three-quarters of the states ratified it, the Nineteenth Amendment was added to the Constitution in 1920.

Women use powerful air-driven hammers to chip away at parts at a Pennsylvania weapons company in 1918. Women hold factory jobs during World War I, but even more worked in traditional "female" occupations, which included teachers, secretaries, and cashiers in shops.

In the meantime, American women were demonstrating their patriotism by filling in for men who went to war. The manpower shortage prompted industries, government agencies, and patriotic groups to urge women to fill the gaps. One poster declared, "Stenographers! Washington needs you." (A stenographer was someone who took down in shorthand the words people said and typed them up later.) "For Every Fighter a Woman Worker," another poster read. A Connecticut weapons factory even had airplanes drop leaflets encouraging women to work.

Women did work during the war, but not in significantly greater numbers compared to the number of working women before the war. (This was true in World War II as well, when more women held skilled jobs than they had before, but the number of women added to the workforce was not much higher than it would have been with young, unmarried women taking jobs.) About one million women in World War I were part of the job force, but the large majority had worked before. They were unmarried women who moved up to better jobs—at least until male soldiers returned—or married women who went back to earn more money while their husbands were away. The big difference was not in numbers but that before the war, most women had worked in "female" occupations—for example, as teachers, housekeepers, cleaners, and

These women, photographed in June 1918, have joined the reserve forces of the U.S. Navy. They are ranked as yeomen—naval personnel who do administrative and clerical work, including managing an office, answering telephones, and handling mail.

seamstresses. During the war they drove streetcars and trucks, assembled airplanes, operated cranes, fixed railroad tracks, welded machinery, and made rubber tires. Even more women worked in offices, as clerks, secretaries, and bookkeepers, or as cashiers in shops or as telephone operators.

Although African American women had a harder time than white women getting these kinds of jobs, many joined the Great Migration and left farming and domestic work for factory jobs and laboring. "We are making more money at this than any work we can get [before the war]. . . . [W]e do not have to work as hard as at housework," said one African American woman who got a job as a railroad worker.

The federal government also needed women to replace men who had gone overseas. Hildegarde Schan was eighteen years old and living in New York when she passed the civil service exam in the fall of 1917. She "got the telegram at one o'clock in the morning for me to report [to Washington, D.C.] on December seventeenth. The next morning, I called them in Washington, and asked if they could wait until after Christmas, you know. And no, they said I had to come right away." Schan was a clerk in the office in charge of storing and supplying weapons. The government "had built a lot of barracks on Pennsylvania Avenue, and that's where we worked, in [a] . . . big, open space." She shared the space with dozens of other women. Although her job in the country's capital ended with the war, she stayed in the civil service, working for the Veterans Bureau (now the Department of Veterans Affairs) back in New York.

Despite increasing the need for their labor on the home front, World War I did not change general attitudes toward women. They would still be paid less and not have the same authority as men. Nor did most of them keep their jobs. "[T]he same patriotism which induced women to enter industry during the war should induce them to vacate their positions after the war," said the Central

Federated Union of New York, which believed, like many Americans, that women should gladly give up their jobs to returning soldiers. By 1920, there was a smaller percentage of women working than there had been in 1910.

Women worked not only on the home front; they also served in the U.S. armed forces. The U.S. Navy made an effort to reach out to women—to employ them in clerical jobs like record keeping, typing, and filing. More than 11,000 women filled these jobs, and almost 270 worked for the U.S. Marines. "I've got the greatest news," wrote Martha L. Wilchinski in a letter to her boyfriend. "Are you ready? Well, then, —I'm a lady leatherneck; . . . I'm a real, live, honest-to-goodness Marine!" Six hundred women turned out with Wilchinski for the first call at a New York City enlistment center. Only three were eventually chosen. But after Wilchinski had begun her service, she wrote another letter: "What'll I say to my grandchildren . . . [w]hen they ask me: 'What did you do in the Great War, Grandma?' I'll have to say: 'Washing windows on the second floor.'"

Female naval personnel and marines were given the same rank as men doing the same jobs—if they were doing the same jobs—although no women were officers. They could also receive veterans' benefits after the war. But the government did not offer them long-term careers in the navy.

The U.S. Army did have a nursing corps, formed in 1898, and more than 21,000 women served in it during World War I. Some were actually in the army; others in fact worked for the American Red Cross. The Red Cross recruited nurses for the army, so often the organization they worked under wasn't clear. About half those nurses served in France. In October 1918, when the Spanish flu epidemic was raging, General Pershing asked for 1,500 additional nurses, instead of more doctors. Nurses might deal with up to fifty patients in a day, working fourteen to eighteen hours. Although more nurses were always needed, only nine African American nurses were accepted to care for soldiers. They worked in Ohio and Illinois, and their only patients were black, not white, men.

More than 200 female Red Cross workers died of influenza. "I felt sick & went to bed about lunch time," wrote one volunteer on a ship filled with soldiers heading toward Europe in October 1918. "Have 'flu,'" she continued, "so frightened. Cannot yet go on deck. Ship still rocks frightfully. . . . Many cases Spanish influenza among privates." Three days later, she recorded, "5 boys dead." By the time the ship landed in France, "Total deaths while on trip were 72." The volunteer survived.

Some nurses in France were members of the U.S. Army; others worked directly for the Red Cross. Here an American Red Cross volunteer, identified as Mrs. Hammond, gives a cup of water to a wounded British soldier on a train platform in Montmirail. This photograph was taken on May 31, 1918.

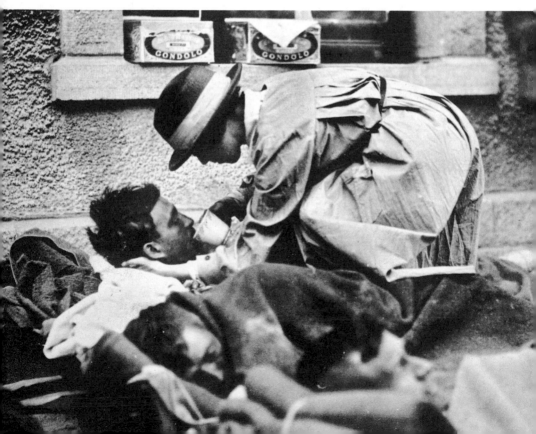

These agricultural workers in the American Women's Land Army farmed in Newton Square, Pennsylvania. The program was modeled on one in Britain and was organized in the United States by women, many of them supporters of suffrage. It brought some 20,000 women from cities and towns to countryside farms to replace men who were in the military. They planted, harvested, plowed, and drove tractors—whatever was needed to keep Americans supplied with food.

Some nurses were stationed at the front to care for the badly wounded and ill who could not be transported behind the lines. They worked in dangerous conditions, sometimes without electricity or water. "Imagine having

280 medical patients and six medicine glasses, no cups or bowls available," wrote one nurse, and later, "I *never* want to see another case of pneumonia following influenza, it is a dreaded disease that is filling our A.E.F. cemetery fast." More than 200 American nurses received decorations for bravery under fire.

Some 6,000 women also did other jobs for the army. Recruited by the Red Cross, as well as by the YWCA and other nonmilitary groups, they, like their civilian counterparts on the home front, were typists, clerks, stenographers who took shorthand, and telephone operators. "For days I was on duty from eight in the morning until ten at night," explained Grace Banker, one of the telephone operators who transmitted calls from the front lines to commanders at headquarters. "[I]t seemed worth while when we gazed at the prison pen filling up with German soldiers."

Some women were translators. Others, called "welfare workers," welcomed and served soldiers at canteens—cafeterias set up by volunteer organizations to give troops a break from the war. They served doughnuts and chatted and danced with soldiers at parties. Only nineteen African American women were accepted to serve with the YMCA in France, running canteens. The canteens for white servicemen had signs that said "No Negroes Allowed." Addie W. Hunton and Kathryn M. Johnson were two of the black volunteers in France. "The fact that prejudice could follow us for three thousand miles across the Atlantic tremendously shocked us," they wrote in a book about their experiences. The injustice "seared . . . [black soldiers'] souls like a hot iron, inflicted as they were at a time when these soldiers were rendering the American army and the nation a sacred service."

Welfare workers like these, as well as clerical workers, wore uniforms and were under the command of army officers, but they were not considered to be officially in the military. They received no veterans' benefits when the war ended; they were just told to go home. In 1979 Congress finally did recognize one group—telephone operators—as members of the U.S. armed forces. Some thirty telephone operators still living were honorably discharged from the army.

Most American women neither worked in factories and offices nor served in the military or as volunteers overseas. They strove to show their patriotism in ways common to women in all wars: they rolled bandages, knitted socks and sweaters, and assembled "comfort kits" for soldiers that included sewing thread, handkerchiefs, writing pads, postcards, buttons, pencils, and Bibles. "The American made wrappings [bandages] etc. are very useful being larger and better than those made in France," wrote a grateful soldier, Francis Erle Cavette.

American women also sent chocolates and cigarettes. At the University of Illinois they formed a chocolate and tobacco fund in September 1917, sending more than 130 boxes of these luxuries to American troops for their first Christmas overseas. F. Lindahl Peterson thanked them: "In a world of rain, discomfort, and work, and where good tobacco is unobtainable, nothing is more highly appreciated than American cigarettes."

More than a million women bought Liberty bonds in the first round of sales—one-third of all the Liberty bonds sold. In an effort to conserve food, they tended victory gardens for their families' use, producing crops worth $350 million ($5.51 billion in today's money) by 1918. In that year, Ida Clyde Clarke published *American Women and the World War*. She focused on the many established and new women's organizations that raised millions of dollars for causes like Belgian refugee relief and the French ambulance service. Clarke described her book as "a story transcribed by me but written in golden deeds by twenty million loyal-hearted women in every state of our great American Union." She wrote the book to record "the actual beginnings of the greatest massed effort of women the world has ever known."

The vast volunteer and work efforts of American women in World War I often went unnoted. After the war, most women returned to their conventional places in the home. They still experienced job discrimination. Their work was valued less than men's. But they did achieve the vote; and, like African Americans, individual women who had participated in the war effort on the home front and in France earned a sense of themselves as capable, valuable human beings.

8

PEACE WITH VICTORY AND A PRICE

There had never been a war like World War I. It took more lives, cost more money, involved more countries, and used more sophisticated and deadly weapons than any other war before it. On November 11, 1918, it ended—that is, the fighting stopped. But many issues remained to be resolved. The German army had been defeated in western Europe but not destroyed. It still controlled part of northeastern France, all of Alsace-Lorraine (which the French thought of as part of their country), and about three-quarters of Belgium. What would happen to Germany and to these areas? What would be the terms of peace?

President Wilson had earlier explained what he thought the terms should

This poster shows Uncle Sam and Lady Liberty walking with the New Year's baby of 1919. The poster celebrates the fact that World War I is over and Americans can look forward to a year of peace and prosperity.

be, almost a year before the end of the war. He said to Congress on January 8, 1918, "What we demand in this war . . . is that the world be made fit and safe to live in; and particularly that it be made safe for every peace-loving nation which, like our own, wishes to live its own life, determine its own institutions, be assured of justice and fair dealing by the other peoples of the world as against force and selfish aggression. All the peoples of the world are in effect partners in this interest, and for our own part we see very clearly that unless justice be done to others it will not be done to us."

Wilson outlined a program for peace that came to be known as "the Fourteen Points." He wanted all the countries at war to negotiate decisions openly without signing secret agreements or treaties with each other. That had been one of the reasons the war had started in the first place. He called for "freedom of navigation upon the seas," free trade between peaceful countries, and a reduction of weapons. Each country would keep only as many weapons as it needed for defense. He wanted colonial peoples to have as much say in their governments as the countries that ruled them. (In this, he was going far beyond the intentions of his allies, Britain and France, which had colonial empires.)

Then Wilson dealt with the actual conditions of the war. Belgium, he said, "must be evacuated [by German troops] and restored, without any attempt to limit the sovereignty which she enjoys in common with all other free nations." Alsace and Lorraine should be returned to France. The various ethnic groups in the Austro-Hungarian Empire should be allowed to develop independently. His fourteenth point understood that to bring the others about: "A general association of nations must be formed under specific covenants for the purpose of affording mutual guarantees of political independence and territorial integrity to great and small states alike." This eventually became the League of Nations.

Wilson concluded, "We have no jealousy of German greatness. . . . We grudge her no achievement or distinction of learning or of pacific [peaceful] enterprise. . . . We do not wish to injure her or to block in any way her legitimate influence or power. We do not wish to fight her either with arms or with hostile arrangements of trade if she is willing to associate herself with us and the other peace-loving nations of the world in covenants [agreements] of justice and law and fair dealing."

"The Big Four"—leaders of the four most prominent Allied Countries (once Russia had dropped out of the war)—meet in Paris in May 1919 for the peace conference that would decide the terms of the treaty to end World War I. They are (*from left to right*): British Prime Minister David Lloyd George, Italian Premier Vittorio Orlando, French Premier Georges Clemenceau, and American President Woodrow Wilson.

In this, he differed from the other Allies, especially France, whose towns and countryside had been destroyed by bombs and battles, with whole villages forever wiped from the earth. Germany, on the other hand, had had almost no fighting on its territory. The French, especially, had deep resentment toward Germany. Germany hoped that peace terms would follow Wilson's plan.

The men who would negotiate peace started talks in Paris on January 19, 1919. Before the armistice Kaiser Wilhelm II had abdicated—given up his position as emperor. Germany had become a republic. Representatives of this new government, not the Kaiser or the military, would settle the peace. Wilson decided to lead the group of Americans who would negotiate. This was unusual. No other American president had traveled to Europe while in office. His supporters urged him to let his representatives handle the negotiations, so he could remain a calm, neutral, wise figure while others debated the details, but he wanted to take part.

In the end, the main negotiations took place between Wilson and the leaders of Britain, France, and Italy. It seemed the four could not agree on anything, including how much to punish Germany by taking her territory, disarming the country, and asking for monetary repayment for damages. The Allied Countries argued over how much new territory each could claim for itself. Britain, with its huge empire and dominance of the sea, had no intention of giving up either. When Wilson went back to the United States from mid-February to mid-March, the American diplomats he left behind to negotiate gave in to most French and British demands. By the time he returned to Europe, the treaty was ready to show to the Germans. It contained 440 sections (called "articles"). The Germans objected to many of them. Nonetheless, Germany, as well as France, Britain, and Italy—and a dissatisfied Wilson—signed what was called "the Treaty of Versailles" (referring to the French palace where the signing took place) on June 28, 1919.

Germany, France, and Britain signed the treaty that ended the war between them on June 28, 1919, in the French palace of Versailles. (President Wilson also signed, although the U.S. Senate never accepted the treaty.) Representatives from each government signed it in the Galerie des Glaces or Hall of Mirrors. The French chose this site because it was the place where Germany had been declared an empire after the French defeat in the Franco-Prussian War. The Treaty of Versailles was only one of the treaties that ended World War I. The United States later made its own peace with the Central Powers.

President Woodrow Wilson steps off a train in Los Angeles on September 19, 1919. The city was one of the stops on his speaking tour to promote the United States joining the League of Nations. About one thousand people came out to greet him at the station. A few days later, Wilson suffered a stroke, and the tour was cancelled. The United States never joined the League of Nations.

Article 231 was the one most hated by Germany. It blamed the country entirely for World War I. It read, "The Allied and Associated Governments affirm and Germany accepts the responsibility . . . for causing all the loss and damage to which the Allied and Associated Governments and their nationals [citizens] have been subjected as a consequence of the war imposed upon them by the aggression of Germany and her allies."

Article 232 was almost as upsetting: "The Allied and Associated Governments . . . require, and Germany undertakes, that she will make compensation for all damage done to the civilian population of the Allied and Associated Powers and to their property during the period of the belligerency. . . ." The treaty actually recognized that Germany had no money itself after the war but insisted on payment for damages anyway, including a first payment of $5 billion ($68.5 billion in today's money). As well as paying for physical destruction, the Germans were to pay veterans' benefits for Allied soldiers who had served in the war. Estimates for how much this would cost reached $100 billion ($1.57 trillion today).

In addition, Germany lost part of its European territory (including Alsace and Lorraine); its overseas colonies; and the use of the Saar Basin—a region of Germany with a very rich coal field—to France for fifteen years. It was to give up most of its weapons or the Allies would occupy the country. The German army could have only 100,000 men, and the navy and air force were also cut back.

Not only Germans but Americans, and certainly Wilson, were upset. The Treaty of Versailles had nothing of the spirit of the Fourteen Points. It was harsh and offended Germany. (Germany would come to ignore many of its provisions.) It did not settle the questions of European dominance, the rights of small as well as large nations to independently decide their governments, the rights of colonies, or freedom of the seas. U.S. Secretary of State Robert Lansing, who had been part of the negotiations, wrote, "The impression made by it [the treaty] is one of disappointment, of regret, and of depression." Many people, including some British and French, believed that the terms of the treaty, including the demand for financial reparations, would in the end lead to another war. They were right. World War II grew out of the unfinished business of World War I that the treaty did not settle, as well as the anger over the treaty in Germany.

One thing that Wilson believed in and fought for, however, was included in the treaty. In fact, it came before the first article as a pledge that any country signing the treaty accepted that: "In order to promote international cooperation and to achieve international peace and security . . . by the prescription of open, just and honourable relations between nations[;] by the firm establishment of the understandings of international law as the actual rule of conduct among Governments, and by the maintenance of justice and a scrupulous respect for all treaty obligations. . . . [We] agree to this Covenant of the League of Nations."

Wilson thought that the League of Nations (like the United Nations today) was essential to preserve peace. This group would resolve disputes between feuding countries before they ever came to war. It could make sure that not only Germany but also other countries limited their weapons. It was a contract for world peace. "[G]o forward," he told Americans, "with lifted eyes and freshened spirit, to follow the vision. . . . The light streams upon the path ahead, and nowhere else." He had an almost religious belief in the importance of the League.

Republicans, who gained a majority in Congress and came to power in 1918, did not agree. Wilson returned to the United States in early July 1919. Other countries had accepted the Treaty of Versailles. The United States had not. It is the Senate's job, not the president's, to agree to the terms of a treaty before it can go into effect. Not just half, but two-thirds of all senators must approve, or ratify, it. The Senate debated for four months, while Wilson toured the country to gather support from the American people. He became ill and, back in Washington, suffered a stroke. A month later, the Senate rejected the treaty twice, and in March 1920, it rejected it again.

Why did the United States not agree to accept the Treaty of Versailles? Most Americans were in favor of it. Even most congressmen were in favor of it. Had the treaty been separate from the League of Nations, the Senate probably would have agreed to it. But the big question was how participating in the League of Nations would affect American foreign policy. Many senators—even Democrats and Wilson supporters—did not want a group of foreign countries to decide how and when the United States should act. Of most concern was article 10: "The Members of the League undertake to respect and preserve as against external aggression the territorial integrity and existing political independence of all Members of the League. In case of any such aggression or in case of any threat or danger of such aggression the Council shall advise upon the means by which this obligation shall be fulfilled."

Did this mean the United States would have to go to war to defend an other country if told to by the League of Nations? Republican Senator Henry Cabot Lodge of Massachusetts, an opponent of the treaty, said, "The United States assumes no obligation to preserve the territorial integrity or political independence of any other country . . . under the provision of Article 10, or to employ the military or naval forces of the United States . . . unless in any particular case the Congress . . . shall . . . so provide." According to the U.S. Constitution, only Congress had the power to declare war. These Republicans and their few Democratic allies viewed the United States as a world leader, as Wilson did. But to them that leadership meant that the United States alone would decide how it should act.

In July 1921, the Senate finally approved its own version of a treaty that ended the United States' war with Germany, Austria, and Hungary. This was separate from the Treaty of Versailles and not signed by the other Allies. The U.S. treaty accepted most of the provisions of Versailles, but it did not obligate the country to join the League of Nations. It never did. Whether or not that made a difference, history proved that the League was unable to preserve peace.

For Home and Country

Alfred Everitt Orr — 18

VICTORY LIBERTY LOAN

9

WAR'S LEGACY

World War I had more impact overseas than it did on the United States' physical territory and economy. No battles took place here, and civilians, except those overseas or on the seas or in a few incidents of sabotage on American soil, were not killed. In addition, the United States had become a nation with financial credits, not debts. The Allied Countries owed America more than $7 billion ($110 billion in today's money). In addition, America advanced the Allies $3 billion ($47 billion today) to recover after the fighting stopped. Because Europe and Britain had relied so heavily on the United States for funding—and because their economies were devastated by the war—America came to replace Britain as the leading economic power in the world. As a participant in the war and the deliberations in Versailles, America assumed a role as one of the world's leaders.

Even after the war ended, the United States needed to raise money. The Allied Countries owed the United States billions of dollars, but they were not able to pay. The government launched a fifth Liberty Loan campaign on April 21, 1919, to sell bonds to the American people. This campaign was called the Victory Liberty Loan, since the United States and its allies had won the war.

The United States had not been a world leader in the nineteenth century. For decades, farming was the main occupation. But by the end of that century more and more Americans were working in cities and factories, producing goods they could sell to Americans and the rest of the world. The country was growing economically stronger year by year. Yet the United States avoided involvement in the wars of Europe or in colonizing the world. It tried to isolate itself, or stay separate, from world politics, even though sometimes it could not. For example, the United States fought wars with Mexico, settled American businesses in Hawaii in the late nineteenth century, and negotiated the end of the 1905 Russo-Japanese War. (Theodore Roosevelt received the Nobel Peace Prize for this. Woodrow Wilson received the same prize in 1919.) Yet isolationism was an important part of American foreign policy.

Just after noon on September 16, 1920, a bomb exploded on Wall Street in New York City, outside banker J. P. Morgan's bank. The bomb was loaded with dynamite and was in a horse-drawn wagon. Almost forty people died, and wreckage filled the streets, as shown in this photograph. While the government eventually suspected Italian anarchists—although some thought the bombers were communists from the Bolshevik Revolution in Russia—no group has ever been held responsible.

While the United States fought the Spanish-American War in 1898—and gained the Philippines and Cuba—it still tended to concentrate on building the U.S. economy and industry and not dealing as a power with the rest of the world.

When World War I began, isolationist feeling was still strong. The fact that the United States officially declared its neutrality instead of taking sides was a sign of this isolation. Many Americans prided themselves on the fact that they were not involved, that they had built a unique country that could continue to prosper without worrying about what was happening overseas.

But the world had changed. The United States was involved, because its economy depended on war business with the Allies. President Wilson saw it in more idealistic terms. The American people "have sought to prepare themselves by the very principles and purposes of their polity [form of government] . . . ," Wilson said in 1917, "ever since the days when they set up a new nation in the high and honorable hope that it might in all that it was and did show mankind the way to liberty." That the United States had a destiny to bring freedom to the world was a popular sentiment of the time.

At the end of the war, many Americans again leaned toward isolationism. The United States had its own problems. In 1919, there were more labor strikes and race riots than there had been before the war. The Communist takeover in Russia encouraged some labor leaders and American socialists to speak out. On the other hand, many Americans feared that communism would take hold in the United States. In the spring of 1919, bombs were sent to several government leaders. Ordinary citizens, seeing no difference between labor unions and radical agitators, attacked both groups (at parades, at rallies, and in their offices) as well as individuals, some of whom were lynched. The federal government did not strongly object to this private violence. When A. Mitchell Palmer became attorney general, he launched a crusade against

The U.S. government formed the World War Foreign Debt Commission on April 18, 1922, to devise a plan for European countries to pay back their World War I debts. Secretary of the Treasury Andrew Mellon (*second from right*) led the group. Herbert Hoover (*far right*), secretary of commerce and future president of the United States, also served on the commission. The United States never recovered all the money owed to it.

all he believed were communists. He had the Federal Bureau of Investigation (FBI) gather information on more than 200,000 organizations and leaders. Because it was easier to deal with foreign-born immigrants, who had fewer rights than American citizens, Palmer went after them. The government raided offices and rounded up supposed communists. The biggest raids, on January 2, 1920, arrested more than 4,000 people in thirty-three cities. Many of these were arrested without warrants. They were detained in centers and sometimes deported—sent back to their home countries.

Palmer went too far in violating civil rights. After objections from Congress, the press, and civil rights organizations, the raids ended. But the use of federal government agencies to seek out disloyalty and censor dissent did not. One of the legacies of World War I was to enhance the role of the Justice Department and the FBI in searching out possible threats to national security, a role that continues to this day. (The federal government bureaucracy also grew; for example, it now had to continue to collect income taxes—taxes Americans pay on the money they earn, which help to pay for defense, education, and other government programs.)

Another less tangible but dangerous result of fear of radicals was that many Americans began to equate demands for workers' and civil rights with being communist and un-American. Fear of immigrants, whether or not they were radical, grew worse after 1919. The Quota Act of 1921, and later the Immigration Act of 1924, limited the number of Italian, Jewish, Russian, eastern European, and many other non–western European immigrants to a few thousand people a year.

Despite some resistance after World War I, the United States could not avoid the fact that much of the rest of the world was devastated and needed help to rebuild. Nor could it ignore its place as the world's economic leader. In fact, the country wanted the power to dominate banking and trade, and to encourage free and open markets ready to buy its goods. This had been one of President Wilson's Fourteen Points. It also insisted that the Allies repay the debts they built up during and after the war—some $10 billion ($137 billion in today's money). But the Allies were broke. The Soviet Union (what Russia had become after the Communist revolution) would not pay the old Russia's debt. Germany, which by the Treaty of Versailles owed the Allies for all the damages war had brought ("reparations"), had less money than Britain and France. What all these countries needed was investment to build up their economies. The United States continued to loan and invest some money in foreign ventures, but it was not enough. Germany used the money it borrowed from American bankers to pay Britain and France, not to build up its own economy. Britain and France then paid that money to the United States. The United States issued more loans to Europe. This was a circle that would have no end.

While the United States' economy grew in the 1920s, European economies did not. The U.S. Congress also passed two tariffs—taxes on goods imported from other countries—in 1922 and 1930. These tariffs protected American manufacturers by making European products more expensive. Americans bought fewer foreign products, thus hurting those economies. Trade slowed nearly to a halt. By 1930, there was a worldwide Depression affecting every country, including the United States. The reasons for the Depression were complex, but one of them was the American financial policy after World War I.

The United States learned again that it could not remain separate from the rest of the world, even though some Americans still supported an isolationist foreign policy. By World War II the country was a political as well as financial leader. But ever since World War I, America's stated reasons for engaging in politics, for going to war, or for taking part in the United Nations have reflected the ideals of Woodrow Wilson. In 2002, President George W. Bush proclaimed the United States should provide the world with "a single sustainable model for national success: freedom, democracy, and free enterprise" and that the "values of freedom are right and true for every person, in every society."

These may be only ideals. They may not be the ideals of the nations we are in conflict with. They may not give us the results that we expect. Countries, including the United States, go to war for many reasons, among them: to maintain their power, protect themselves from foreign invasion, keep control over other countries they traditionally dominate, improve their economies, and

After twenty months of war, Americans were excited to see World War I end. This celebration of the armistice took place on Wall Street in New York City on December 5, 1918. But the legacy of our involvement in the war has lasted into the twenty-first century. The United States became an economic and political global power that still exerts tremendous influence on world events and policies today.

spread their religious beliefs. Americans still question whether the United States should—or even can—take on trouble spots all over the world. Perhaps there will always be reasons to go to war, but there will also be valid reasons not to. The debate between personal freedom and national security continues.

Today, as the country faces terrorist threats, American leaders again echo the words of Wilson. "Just as we stood for freedom in the twentieth century, we must stand together for the right of people everywhere to live free from fear in the twenty-first century," said President Barack Obama in 2009. Addressing a group of South American leaders in 2011, he added: "We're people of faith who must remember that all of us—especially the most fortunate among us—must do our part, especially for the least among us. We're citizens who know that ensuring that democracies deliver for our people must be the work of all. This is our common history. This is our common heritage."

Other countries look to the United States for support and guidance, or seek to undermine or destroy us, because we have influence, and because we are a world power. This is the legacy of World War I.

The District of Columbia War Memorial was dedicated and opened on November 11, 1931, exactly thirteen years after the armistice. The names of 499 Washington, D.C., residents who died in the war are carved into its base. Many towns and cities in the United States and Europe built monuments, large and small, to honor those who fought in World War I and to preserve their memory.

Time Line of Key Events

1913

March 4   Woodrow Wilson is sworn in as the 28th president of the United States.

1914

June 28   Archduke Franz Ferdinand, heir to the Austro-Hungarian Empire, is assassinated by a Serbian nationalist in Sarajevo, Bosnia.

July 28   Austria-Hungary declares war on Serbia.

July 30   Russia begins mobilizing troops to fight Austria-Hungary and its ally, Germany.

August 1   Germany declares war on Russia.

August 3   Germany declares war on France, Russia's ally.

August 4   Germany invades neutral Belgium on its way to France; Britain declares war on Germany in response to Belgian invasion.

August 19   President Wilson declares to the U.S. Senate that the United States will remain neutral as Europe fights.

Sept. 6–12   First Battle of the Marne; France and Britain stop German advance into France.

November 3   Britain begins to mine North Sea to prevent German trade.

1915

January 10   Woman's Peace Party is organized, with activist Jane Addams as its head.

February 4   Germany declares that the sea around Britain is a war zone, where ships can be torpedoed by German submarines.

March   The British navy builds up a total blockade to keep ships from delivering supplies to Germany. The blockade will prove very effective, nearly starving the German people as the war goes on.

World War I began in Europe three years before the United States entered the war. These French tanks are passing through the village of Rampant, likely on their way to battle.

April 26	Italy agrees to join the war on the Allied side, largely to fight Austria-Hungary, whose land it borders.
May 7	A German submarine, *U-20*, sinks the passenger ship *Lusitania*, with the loss of 128 American lives.
May 10	Instead of declaring war on Germany, Wilson makes a speech that says the United States will not join the fight.
May 13	The United States sends a diplomatic note to Germany asking the Germans to call off submarine warfare in neutral waters.
June 9	The United States sends a second diplomatic note to Germany.
July 21	The United States sends a firm third note to Germany, saying that it will consider any more torpedoing of ships headed to Britain "deliberately unfriendly."
August 10	The first military training camp for civilians opens in Plattsburgh, New York.
August 19	A German submarine sinks the *Arabic*, killing two Americans.
September 1	Germany pays for the damage and deaths caused when the *Arabic* sank. It agrees to limits on submarine warfare.
November 1	The pacifist Anti-Preparedness Committee organizes.
November 4	President Wilson asks Congress to enlarge the U.S. Army and Navy.

American soldiers load a mobile railroad gun, which shoots shells that measure more than one foot in diameter. They are at the Argonne front in Baleycourt, France, in November 1918.

During the third Liberty Loan campaign, these members of "the Liberty Loan Choir" sing on the steps of City Hall in New York City. Crowds of Americans came to be entertained and to buy Liberty bonds.

1916

February 8	Germany again authorizes its submarines to torpedo armed merchant ships.
February 21	Battle of Verdun begins. It lasts until December 18.
March–April	Britain tightens its naval blockade around Germany.
March 9	Pancho Villa's Mexican troops attack Columbus, New Mexico.
March 15	The United States sends 11,000 soldiers into Mexico under General John J. Pershing to capture Villa.
March 24	A German submarine sinks the French ship *Sussex*. Some Americans are hurt.
April 24	Irish nationalists rebel against British rule in Ireland in the Easter Rebellion. Britain represses the rebellion. Many Irish Americans are upset and become anti-British.
June 3	Congress passes the National Defense Act, which increases the size of the U.S. Army.
July 1	Battle of the Somme begins. It ends on November 18.
July 30	An explosion in New Jersey destroys huge numbers of weapons waiting to be shipped to the Allies. German agents and German Americans are suspected.
August 29	Congress passes the Naval Act, which calls for building new battleships and destroyers.

| November 7 | Woodrow Wilson wins election to a second term as president of the United States. He wins on the slogan "He kept us out of war." |
| December 18 | President Wilson calls on the warring countries on both sides to say what terms they would require for peace. |

1917

January 10	The National Women's Party, the more militant of suffragist organizations, begins picketing the White House to demand votes for women.
January 22	President Wilson makes a speech calling for "peace without victory," meaning the war could stop before one side or the other in Europe was completely destroyed.
January 31	Germany declares that it will pursue unrestricted submarine warfare, making any ship, neutral or not, a target.
February 3	The United States, no longer neutral, breaks off diplomatic relations with Germany.
February 5	The U.S. Army leaves Mexico, having failed to capture Pancho Villa. But American troops gain some experience in warfare that will be useful when they enter World War I.
February 28	President Wilson informs the American press of the Zimmermann Telegram from the Foreign Secretary of Germany to Mexico, calling on the country to ally with Germany.
March 12	President Wilson orders that all U.S. merchant ships be armed with weapons.
April 2	President Wilson asks Congress to declare war on Germany.
April 6	Congress declares war on Germany.
April 13	The federal government establishes the Committee on Public Information (CPI), headed by George Creel.
May 10	British and American ships begin a convoy system; several ships—some armed—travel together to protect themselves from German submarines.
May 12	President Wilson appoints General John Pershing to head the American Expeditionary Force (AEF), the army that the United States sends to France.

May 18	President Wilson signs the Selective Service Act, calling for registration and drafting of young men. Registration begins on June 5.
June 15	Congress passes the Espionage Act, giving the federal government censorship powers.
June 20	The first Liberty loan drive is launched.
June 26	The first American soldiers arrive in France.
July 1	The Civil Liberties Bureau is founded. It will become the American Civil Liberties Union, which is still active today.
July 12	Striking copper miners in Bisbee, Arizona, are arrested and sent by train to the desert.
July 21	Battle of Passchendaele begins. It is over on November 6.
August 23	Black troops attack white civilians in Houston, Texas, enraged by segregation practices.
September 5	The federal government begins raids on the offices of the radical union the Industrial Workers of the World (IWW).
October 24	Battle of Caporetto begins, pitting Italians against German and Austro-Hungarian troops. It ends in November with Italy's defeat. Italy calls on the other Allies for help.
November 7	Communists assume power in Russia.

1918

January 8	President Wilson delivers his "Fourteen Points" speech to Congress.
March 3	Russia and Germany sign the Treaty of Brest-Litovsk, ending their war.
March 11	First reports of the Spanish influenza outbreak are issued in Fort Riley, Kansas.
April 1	The German army begins an offensive attack against the Allies along the Somme River.
April 5	German immigrant Robert Prager is lynched in Illinois; he is believed to be a spy. He is not.
May 16	Congress passes the Sedition Act, which establishes grounds for censorship and imprisonment, in addition to those listed in the Espionage Act.

This American officer rides in the basket of an observation balloon in April 1918. He flies over enemy territory near the front lines to report back on German army movement and activities.

May 27   The German army launches an attack along the Aisne River. By May 31, it will reach the Marne River, within potential striking distance of Paris.

May 28   The U.S. Army experiences its first battle at Cantigny.

June 3–4   Americans participate in their first major action, helping to stop the Germans at Château-Thierry.

June 6–26   American soldiers and marines take part in extensive fighting at Belleau Wood.

June 16   In Ohio socialist Eugene Debs gives a speech that includes remarks against the imprisonment of antiwar demonstrators. Two weeks later he is arrested under the Espionage Act, and in September he is sentenced to ten years in jail. (The sentence is commuted in 1921.)

July 18   The Allied armies, including 310,000 American troops, launch the Aisne-Marne offensive attack. The offensive ends on August 6.

August 16	The first American troops arrive in Vladivostok, Russia.
Sept. 12–15	U.S. and French troops attack and capture the Saint-Mihiel salient.
September 26	U.S. forces launch the Meuse-Argonne offensive.
October 16	Congress passes the Immigration Act, making it easier to deport suspected immigrant radicals.
November 5	In the congressional elections, the Republicans win a majority. They will oppose President Wilson's peace settlement plans.
November 9	Kaiser Wilhelm II abdicates as leader of Germany and flees to neutral Netherlands. (He dies there in 1941.)
November 11	An armistice is declared between the Allies and Germany.

1919

January 18	The Peace Conference opens in Paris. President Wilson attends.
February 15	President Wilson returns to the United States for several weeks.
June 4	Congress passes the 19th Amendment to the Constitution, giving women the right to vote. It is finally ratified by enough states and goes into effect August 26, 1920.
June 28	Germany, France, and Britain sign the Treaty of Versailles, ending war between them. President Wilson also signs, but the treaty is not valid until ratified by the Senate.
July 9	The German government ratifies the treaty.
July 10	President Wilson presents the treaty to the U.S. Senate. The Senate needs to approve it by a two-thirds majority vote for it to go into effect.
August 21	President Wilson shuts down the Committee on Public Information.
September 3	Wilson begins a speaking tour of the United States to promote ratifying the Treaty of Versailles and joining the League of Nations.
September 25	President Wilson collapses while in Colorado and returns to Washington.
October 2	Wilson has a stroke. His health will be poor throughout the rest of his term as president.
November 19	The U.S. Senate rejects the Treaty of Versailles. This is the first time in the Senate's history that it rejects a peace treaty.

1920

January 2   Government officials round up an estimated 3,000–10,000 suspected radicals, including communists and labor agitators.

March 19   The U.S. Senate rejects the Treaty of Versailles for a second time.

November 2   Republican Warren Harding is elected U.S. president. He will take over in March 1921.

December 10   Woodrow Wilson is awarded the 1919 Nobel Peace Prize.

December 13   Congress repeals the Sedition Act.

1921

July 2   A joint resolution by the U.S. Senate and House of Representatives declares that the war with Germany and Austria-Hungary is over.

October 18   The U.S. Senate ratifies separate treaties between the United States and Germany and Austria.

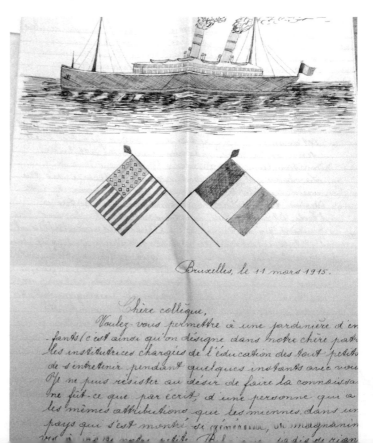

A Belgian child wrote this letter to President Wilson in 1915 to thank Americans for sending food and other aid to Belgium after Germany invaded. It shows a ship that carries goods and the American and Belgian flags crossed in friendship.

154

Notes

*Full bibliographic information for books cited in the Notes
can be found in the Selected Bibliography.*

Note on the title

The phrase "Come On In, America" is taken from an anti-war cartoon by
M. A. Kempf, published in the magazine *The Masses* in June 1917. The entire
title is "Come On In America, the Blood's Fine." It shows a grim, frightening-
looking man who represents war pulling three women—England, France, and
Germany—into a pool of blood. The cartoon vividly shows the horrors of
war, which were terrible. Many Americans supported World War I, but there
were also people who opposed it, both before and after we entered.

Introduction

page 2 "we will not . . . at last free." http://wwi.lib.byu.edu/index.php/
Wilson's_War_Message_to_Congress (accessed February 26, 2016).

page 2 Death statistics. https://www.pbs.org/greatwar/resources/
casdeath_pop.html (accessed February 14, 2016).

Chapter 1: War Begins in Europe

page 7 "Heir to . . . in a heap." http://chroniclingamerica.loc.gov/lccn/
sn83030214/1914-06-29/ed-1/seq-1/ (accessed February 17,
2016).

page 13 "Germany endeavored . . . until today." Carlisle, *World War I*, p. 25.

pages 13–14 "Paris went on . . . was ready." Ibid.

page 14 "Hardly anyone . . . astonishment." Englund, *Beauty and the Sorrow*,
pp. 10–11.

Chapter 2: The United States Stays Neutral—or Does It?

page 20 Until 1951, the city of Plattsburgh, New York, used the spelling

"Plattsburg," as on the poster. The correct spelling now is "Plattsburgh," used throughout this book.

page 22   "neutral . . . action." Zieger, *America's Great War*, p. 7.

pages 22–23   On U.S. percentage of world trade. Ibid, p. 10.

page 24   "bound together . . . purpose." Doenecke, *Nothing Less Than War*, p. 22.

page 24   "a big dog . . . little one." Ibid, p. 28.

page 24   "three days . . . and sky." Ibid.

pages 25–26   "It was . . . overturned lifeboats." Zieger, *America's Great War*, p. 22.

page 26   *Lusitania* statistics. Bausum, *Unraveling Freedom*, p. 23.

page 27   "acceptance by . . . time of war." https://as205.omeka.net/exhibits/show/tr232/item/133 (accessed March 3, 2016).

page 27   "In the present . . . move westward." Nelson, *Five Lieutenants*, pp. 8–9.

page 29   "We are a committee . . . ill-considered action." Bennett and Howlett, *Antiwar Dissent*, pp. 39–40.

page 29   "There were no bands . . . on the beholders." http://broom02.revolvy.com/main/index.php?s=Woman%27s%20Peace%20Party&item_type=topic (accessed February 28, 2016).

pages 29–30   "As women . . . destruction." Bennett and Howlett, *Antiwar Dissent*, p. 37.

page 31   "a peace without . . . principles." Keene, *United States and the First World War*, p. 16.

page 33   "on the following . . . and Arizona." https://www.archives.gov/education/lessons/zimmermann/ (accessed February 26, 2016).

page 34   "It would seem . . . independence." Kennedy, *Over Here*, p. 37.

page 34   "How is it . . . on the brink of." Bennett and Howlett, *Antiwar Dissent*, p. 77.

page 35   "The question is . . . for efficiency." Kennedy, *Over Here*, p. 43.

Chapter 3: The United States Joins the Fight

page 37   "Good Lord! . . . are you?" Keene, *World War I*, p. 11.

pages 37–38   Statistics for U.S. troops. http://www.archives.gov/publications/prologue/1998/fall/military-service-in-world-war-one.html (accessed March 12, 2016).

page 38   "We men . . . pass it up." Nelson, *Five Lieutenants*, p. 31.

page 38 "What actuated . . . at stake." Ibid, p. 46, 78.

page 38 "The whole nation . . . to call him." http://www.firstworldwar.com/source/usconscription_wilson.html (accessed March 12, 2016).

page 39 "still strongly . . . abolished." http://wwvets.com/MedicalCorps.html (accessed May 6, 2016).

page 40 "Soldiering . . . your own." Rubin, *Last of the Doughboys*, p. 13.

page 40 Origins of "doughboy." http://www.worldwar1.com/dbc/origindb.htm (accessed March 4, 2016).

page 41 Statistics on U.S. Navy. Keene, *World War I*, p. 125.

page 42 "54 degrees . . . funnels were bent." http://www.wwvets.com/navy.html (accessed April 28, 2016).

pages 42–43 "We made . . . not at home." http://www.wwvets.com/army.html (accessed April 28, 2016).

pages 43–44 "very old . . . on the floor." Nelson, *Five Lieutenants*, p. 67.

pages 44–45 "The shells . . . and exploded." Rubin, *Last of the Doughboys*, pp. 22–23.

page 45 "The horror . . . so short a time." Doenecke, *Nothing Less Than War*, p. 32.

pages 45–46 "I will try . . . with four men." https://jaclynhughes.files.wordpress.com/2014/12/ww1-personal-story-peter-schaming.pdf (accessed July 6, 2016).

page 46 Losses at Battle of the Somme. Keene, *World War I*, p. 12.

page 47 "could only stagger . . . asleep." Keene, *United States and the First World War*, p. 56.

page 49 "They started . . . woods, fighting." Rubin, *Last of the Doughboys*, pp. 190, 192.

page 49 Casualties at Belleau Wood. Ibid, p. 193.

page 50 "On the 18th . . . three days." Zieger, *America's Great War*, p. 98.

page 51 "saw a sight . . . earth quake." Kennedy, *Over Here*, p. 193.

page 51 "everything is . . . 60 deaths." Zieger, *America's Great War*, p. 109.

page 52 "memorable day . . . FINIS LE GUERRE." http://libcdm1.uncg.edu/cdm/fullbrowser/collection/WVHP/id/2110/rv/compoundobject/cpd/2193/rec/1 (accessed March 1, 2016).

page 52 "You cannot imagine . . . *Star Spangled Banner*." George, *World War I*, p. 77.

Chapter 4: New and Improved Weapons

page 56 "Those who knew . . . giant artillery." http://www.oldmagazinearticles .com/draw_pdf.php?filename=Bartlett.pdf (accessed April 28, 2016).

page 56 Number of horses killed at Verdun. Gilbert, *First World War*, p. 235.

page 56 "in the infantry . . . to perfect him." http://www.oldmagazinearticles .com/draw_pdf.php?filename=Bartlett.pdf (accessed April 28, 2016).

page 57 Number of shells at Battle of the Marne. http://www.smithsonianmag .com/history/the-shock-of-war-55376701/?no-ist (accessed April 28, 2016).

pages 57–58 "There was a sound . . . as a small room." Ibid.

page 58 "at three o'clock . . . on top of us." Sheffield, *War on the Western Front*, p. 23.

page 58 "twenty-four . . . disturbance." Englund, *Beauty and the Sorrow*, p. 486.

page 59 "was quite . . . line of duty." Ibid, pp. 489–90.

page 60 "assigned to a . . . the trenches." http://www.wwvets.com/ MachineGunners.html (accessed May 2, 2016).

pages 60–61 "highly praised . . . functioned well." Sheffield, *War on the Western Front*, p. 250.

page 62 "The defenders . . . [smoke]." Ibid, p. 212.

pages 62–63 "queer, greenish-yellow . . . on the spot." http://chemicalweapons .cenmag.org/when-chemicals-became-weapons-of-war/ (accessed May 9, 2016).

page 63 Statistics on shells filled with gas. Keene, *World War I*, p. 142.

page 64 "Gas travels . . . of the chemicals." http://www.eyewitnesstohistory .com/gas.htm (accessed May 9, 2016).

page 65 Deaths from mustard gas. http://chemicalweapons.cenmag.org/ when-chemicals-became-weapons-of-war/ (accessed May 9, 2016).

page 65 "Life in the . . . external armor." http://www.wwvets.com/Tanks.html (accessed May 2, 2016).

page 66 "As we approached . . . nothing at all." Sheffield, *War on the Western Front*, p. 260.

pages 66–67 "The English . . . a chance." Englund, *Beauty and the Sorrow*, p. 367.

pages 67–68 "At 150 yards . . . into the ground." Grant, *Definitive Visual History*, p. 297.

page 68 Statistics on bombs dropped on London. Gilbert, *First World War*, pp. 339–40.

page 69   "bunk was too small . . . damp cellar." http://www.vlib.us/wwi/ resources/archives/texts/uboatu9.html (accessed May 12, 2016).

Chapter 5: The War on Our Home Front

page 72   Statistics on trade and income. https://sites.google.com/site/ wartoendallwarscom/home/industry-during-ww1 (accessed April 28, 2016).

pages 72–73   Statistics on employment. http://www.nber.org/digest/jan05/ w10580.html (accessed April 28, 2016).

pages 74–75   "Go back . . . by all means." Zieger, *America's Great War*, p. 74.

page 75   "SAVE WHEAT . . . I'll wait." https://www.ourcomestories.com/ asset/view/CONSERVING-FOOD-IN-WWI-Children in War (accessed May 6, 2016).

page 76   "It has been demonstrated . . . they did fencing." Blatch, *Mobilizing Woman-Power*, pp. 166–67.

page 76   "Guess you have . . . store closed." George, *World War I*, p. 26.

page 78   "We went direct . . . human motives" Kennedy, *Over Here*, p. 105.

page 79   "There was a . . . a few bonds." George, *World War I*, p. 32.

page 79   "A man . . . American citizen." Kennedy, *Over Here*, p. 106.

page 79   "I have been in . . . not be helped." Bennett and Howlett, *Antiwar Dissent*, p. 123.

page 81   "imagination . . . same way." Kennedy, *Over Here*, p. 55.

page 83   "The speech must not . . . worth fighting for.'" http:// historymatters.gmu.edu/d/4970/ (accessed March 10, 2016).

page 83   On CPI output. Kennedy, *Over Here*, p. 61.

pages 83–84   "THE authentic record . . . patriotic citizen." http://memory.loc.gov/ diglib/vhp/story/loc.natlib.afc2001001.28523/ pageturner?ID=pm0001001 (accessed February 25, 2016).

page 84   "If there should be . . . stern repression." http://wwi.lib.byu.edu/index .php/Wilson's_War_Message_to_Congress. (accessed February 26, 2016).

page 84   "has all the earmarks . . . and patriotism." Feldman, *Manufacturing Hysteria*, p. 32.

page 84   "Every letter . . . nonmailable." Keene, *United States and the First World War*, p. 99.

page 85 "interfere . . . forces." Ibid.

page 86 "I . . . planned . . . war and after." Bennett and Howlett, *Antiwar Dissent*, p. 131.

page 86 "any disloyal . . . the Constitution." Keene, *United States and the First World War*, p. 99.

page 87 "The working class . . . does both." Bennett and Howlett, *Antiwar Dissent*, pp. 92–93.

page 88 "material . . . Espionage Act." Kennedy, *Over Here*, p. 65.

page 88 Number of foreign-born in U.S. armed forces. Keene, *United States and the First World War*, p. 60.

pages 90–91 "It is our earnest . . . give like service." Bennett and Howlett, *Antiwar Dissent*, pp. 74–75.

page 91 On number of strikers. Zieger, *America's Great War*, p. 117.

page 92 "the IWW agitators . . . the United States." Kennedy, *Over Here*, p. 73.

page 92 "Two sons . . . those early days." https://www.loc.gov/resource/wpalh3.33020106/?sp=6 (accessed May 11, 1016).

page 92 "It is still a question . . . your decision." George, *World War I*, p. 45.

pages 92–93 "Those who opposed . . . German submarines." Bennett and Howlett, *Antiwar Dissent*, p. 126.

page 93 "I am not seeking . . . the same end—war." Roger Baldwin quoted in Ibid, pp. 190–91.

page 93 "punished . . . for three days." Ibid, p. 197.

Chapter 6: African Americans at War and at Home

page 97 "Young negro men . . . we get nothing." Bennett and Howlett, *Antiwar Dissent*, p. 173.

page 98 "Negro enlistment was discouraged." Rubin, *Last of the Doughboys*, p. 261.

page 98 "arrogant . . . community." Kennedy, *Over Here*, p. 159.

page 98 "Let us not . . . to the hills." Zieger, *America's Great War*, pp. 130–31.

page 100 "though we carried . . . of the procession." Osborne, *Miles to Go for Freedom*, p. 80.

page 100 "felt that I . . . of Democracy." http://exhibitions.nypl.org/africanaage/essay-world-war-i.html (accessed April 19, 2016).

pages 101   "I remember the day . . . November 1917." Horace Pippin, lightly edited for readability, at http://www.aaa.si.edu/collections/viewer/horace-pippin-memoir-his-experiences-world-war-i-7434 (accessed April 26, 2016), p. 1. (Page numbers indicate the page in Pippin's handwritten manuscript where quotes are found.)

pages 101–2   "laid about five hundred . . . go to bed wet." Ibid, pp. 3–4.

page 102   "I remember . . . went to bed wet." Ibid, p. 7.

page 102   "gave us shell fire . . . their shells." Ibid, pp. 11-12.

page 103   "must not eat . . . white Americans." http://edsitement.neh.gov/lesson-plan/african-american-soldiers-world-war-i-92nd and 93rd-divisions (accessed April 26, 2016).

page 104   "There were . . . day after tomorrow. http://forlorn.library.org/overview/Harlem_Hellfighters.html (accessed April 28, 2016).

page 104   "Stones, dirt . . . near you." Ibid.

pages 104–5   "While on night . . . until they retreated." https://www.army.mil/medalofhonor/johnson/ (accessed May 11, 2016).

page 105   "I cannot commend . . . dangerous work." http://edsitement.neh.gov/lesson-plan/african-american-soldiers-world-war-i-92nd-and-93rd-divisions (accessed April 26, 2016).

page 105   "That day, the sun . . . New York Infantry." http://www.npr.org/sections/codeswitch/2014/04/01/294913379/the-harlem-hellfighters-fighting-racism-in-the-trenches-of-wwi (accessed May 11, 2016).

pages 105–7   "There is no advancement . . . make good." Grossman, *Chance to Make Good*, pp. 104–5.

page 106   On number of African Americans in Great Migration. Zieger, *America's Great War*, p. 128.

page 107   "Because Negroes . . . long one." George, *World War I*, p. 56.

page 107   "that had no water . . . flooded." Ibid, p. 129.

page 107   "Negroes were coming . . . closer and closer." George, *World War I*, p. 59.

pages 107–8   Statistics on lynching. Zieger, *America's Great War*, p. 128.

page 108   "lynching is . . . of this kind." Ibid.

pages 108–9   "Optimism . . . will not happen." Bennett and Howlett, *Antiwar Dissent*, p. 183.

page 110 "I had a nice uniform . . . down the streets here." Reisman, *I Feel So Good*, p. 34.

page 110 "You know now . . . real American men." Keene, *United States and the First World War*, p. 63.

page 110 "We *return* . . . the reason why." Dailey, *Age of Jim Crow*, pp. 128–29.

Chapter 7: Women, Suffrage, and Service

pages 113–14 "inspire, encourage . . . critical hour." Keene, *World War I*, pp. 113–14.

page 114 "Rise up, women . . . goes marching on." http://thesuffragettes.org/resources/anthems/ (accessed May 12, 2016).

pages 115–16 On the arrest of women picketers. Carlisle, *World War I*, p. 233.

page 116 "As long as . . . go to jail." http://www.novahistory.org/Lorton_Womens_Suffrage.htm (accessed May 12, 2016).

page 116 "announced . . . the nose." Ibid.

page 116 "is vital . . . the war." Kennedy, *Over Here*, p. 284.

page 119 "We are making . . . housework." Zieger, *America's Great War*, p. 145.

page 119 "got the telegram . . . right away." Rubin, *Last of the Doughboys*, p. 389.

page 119 "had built . . . open space." Ibid, p. 392.

page 119 "The same patriotism . . . after the war." Kennedy, *Over Here*, p. 285.

page 120 On number of women in U.S. armed forces. Zieger, *America's Great War*, p. 142.

page 120 "I've got the greatest . . . Marine!" George, *World War I*, p. 68.

page 120 "What'll I say . . . second floor." Ibid, p. 69.

page 121 "I felt sick . . . were 72." http://libcdm1.uncg.edu/cdm/compoundobject/collection/WVHP/id/2193/rec/21 (accessed April 12, 2016).

pages 122–23 "Imagine having . . . cemetery fast." Keene, *World War I*, p. 116.

page 124 "For days I was . . . German soldiers." Ibid, pp. 118–19.

page 124 "The fact that prejudice . . . sacred service." George, *World War I*, p. 72.

page 125 "The American made . . . made in France." http://archives.library.illinois.edu/blog/red-cross/ (accessed April 12, 2016).

page 125 "In a world . . . cigarettes." Ibid.

page 125 "a story transcribed . . . ever known." http://www.gwpda.org/
wwi-www/Clarke/Clarke00TC.htm (accessed April 14, 2016).

Chapter 8: Peace with Victory and a Price

page 128 "What we demand . . . done to us." http://avalon.law.yale.edu/20th_
century/wilson14.asp (accessed March 2, 2016).

page 128 "must be evacuated . . . free nations." Ibid.

page 128 "A general association . . . states alike." Ibid.

page 129 "We have no jealousy . . . fair dealing." Ibid.

page 132 "The Allied and Associated Governments affirm . . . the allies." Ibid.

pages 132–33 "The Allied and Associated Governments affirm . . . her belligerency." Ibid.

page 133 "The impression . . . depression." Zieger, *America's Great War*, p. 103.

page 134 "In order to promote . . . League of Nations." http://avalon.law.yale
.edu/imt/parti.asp (accessed March 2, 2016).

page 134 "Go forward . . . nowhere else." Zieger, *America's Great War*, pp. 184–85.

page 135 "The Members . . . shall be fulfilled." http://avalon.law.yale.edu/imt/
parti.asp (accessed March 2, 2016).

page 135 "The United States assumes . . . so provide." Zieger, *America's Great War*,
p. 221.

Chapter 9: War's Legacy

page 139 "have sought to prepare . . . way to liberty." Kennedy, *Over Here*, p. 383.

page 142 "a single sustainable . . . in every society." Ibid, pp. 389–90.

page 144 "Just as we stood . . . the twenty-first century." https://www.whitehouse
.gov/issues/foreign-policy/cross-cutting-issues (accessed March 30,
2016).

page 144 "We're people of faith . . . common heritage." https://www
.whitehouse.gov/issues/foreign-policy#section-middle-east-and-
north-africa (accessed July 6, 2016).

Selected Bibliography

* Indicates books suitable for young readers

* Adams, Simon. *Eyewitness World War I*. New York: DK, 2014.

* Barber, Nicola. *World War I*. Chicago: Heinemann Library, 2012.

* Bausum, Ann. *Unraveling Freedom: The Battle for Democracy on the Home Front During World War I*. Washington, D.C.: National Geographic, 2010.

Bennett, Scott H., and Charles F. Howlett, eds. *Antiwar Dissent and Peace Activism in World War I America: A Documentary Reader*. Lincoln, Neb.: University of Nebraska Press, 2014.

Blatch, Harriet Stanton. *Mobilizing Woman-Power*. New York: The Womans Press, 1918.

Carlisle, Rodney P. *World War I*. New York: Facts on File, 2007.

Dailey, Jane, ed. *The Age of Jim Crow*. New York: W. W. Norton, 2009.

Doenecke, Justus D. *Nothing Less Than War: A New History of America's Entry into World War I*. Lexington, Ken.: University Press of Kentucky, 2011.

* Dolan, Edward F. *America in World War I*. Brookfield, Conn.: Millbrook Press, 1996.

Englund, Peter. *The Beauty and the Sorrow: An Intimate History of the First World War*. Peter Graves, trans. New York: Vintage Books, 2012.

Feldman, Jay. *Manufacturing Hysteria: A History of Scapegoating, Surveillance, and Secrecy in Modern America*. New York: Anchor Books, 2012. (First published in 2011.)

* Freedman, Russell. *The War to End All Wars: World War I*. Boston: Houghton Mifflin Harcourt, 2010.

* George, Linda S. *World War I: Letters from the Homefront*. New York: Benchmark Books, 2002.

Gilbert, Martin. *The First World War: A Complete History*, 2nd ed. New York: Henry Holt and Company, 2004.

Grant, R. G. *World War I: The Definitive Visual History*. New York: DK, 2014.

* Grossman, James R. *A Chance to Make Good: African Americans, 1900–1929*. New York: Oxford University Press, 1997.

Keegan, John. *The First World War*. New York: Vintage Books, 2000. (First published in 1998.)

Keene, Jennifer D. *Doughboys, the Great War, and the Remaking of America*. Baltimore: Johns Hopkins University Press, 2006. (First published in 2001.)

———. *The United States and the First World War*. Harlow, England: Pearson Education, 2000.

———. *World War I: The American Soldier Experience*. Lincoln, Neb.: University of Nebraska Press, 2011. (First published in 2006.)

Kennedy, David M. *Over Here: The First World War and American Society*. New York: Oxford University Press, 1980.

Kerr, Gordon. *A Short History of the First World War: Land, Sea & Air, 1914–1918*. Harpenden, England: Pocket Essentials, 2014.

MacMillan, Margaret. *The War That Ended Peace: The Road to 1914*. New York: Random House, 2014.

Nelson, James Carl. *Five Lieutenants: The Heartbreaking Story of Five Harvard Men Who Led America to Victory in World War I*. New York: St. Martin's Press, 2012.

*Osborne, Linda Barrett. *Miles to Go for Freedom: Segregation & Civil Rights in the Jim Crow Years*. New York: Abrams / Washington, D.C.: Library of Congress, 2012.

* Pratt, Mary K. *World War I*. Minneapolis: Abdo Publishing Company, 2014.

Reisman, Bob. *I Feel So Good: The Life and Times of Big Bill Broonzy*. Chicago: University of Chicago Press, 2011.

Rubin, Richard. *The Last of the Doughboys: The Forgotten Generation and Their Forgotten World War*. Boston: Hougton Mifflin Harcourt, 2013.

Sheffield, Gary D. *War on the Western Front*. London: Bounty Books, 2014.

Wagner, Margaret E. *America and the Great War: A Library of Congress Illustrated History*. New York: Bloomsbury Press, 2017.

Zieger, Robert H. *America's Great War: World War I and the American Experience*. Lanham, Md.: Rowman & Littlefield, 2000.

Image Credits

Page vi: Library of Congress LC-USZC4-7753. **Page 3:** National Archives photo no. War and Conflict 695. **Page 5:** Library of Congress LC-DIG-ppmsca-40046. **Page 6:** Library of Congress LC-USZC4-10881. **Page 9:** Library of Congress LC-DIG-ggbain-15555. **Page 15:** Library of Congress LC-DIG-ggbain-16893. **Page 16:** Library of Congress LC-DIG-ggbain-17578. **Page 19:** National Archives. 165-WW-558C(3). **Page 20:** Library of Congress LC-USZC4-9021. **Page 22:** Library of Congress LC-DIG-ggbain-25318. **Page 25:** Library of Congress LC-USZC4-13285. **Page 28:** Library of Congress LC-DIG-ggbain-29656. **Page 30:** Library of Congress LC-DIG-ggbain-18848. **Page 32:** Harry S. Truman Library and Museum. **Page 33:** Library of Congress LC-USZ62-42297. **Page 36:** Library of Congress LC-USZC4-9016. **Page 39:** Library of Congress LC-DIG-ggbain-24282. **Page 40:** Courtesy National Archives. 111-SC-36202. **Page 41:** Courtesy National Archives photo no. 165-WW-289C-007. **Page 44:** Courtesy National Archives photo no. 165-WW- 463A(51). **Page 46:** Library of Congress LC-DIG-stereo-1s04035. **Page 47:** Courtesy National Archives photo no. 111-SC-16352. **Page 48:** Library of Congress LC-USZ62-39182. **Page 49:** Courtesy National Archives photo no. 111-SC-94980. **Page 53:** Courtesy National Archives photo no. 111-SC-33075. **Page 54:** Library of Congress LC-USZC4-5869. **Page 57:** Library of Congress LC-DIG-ggbain-24636. **Page 59:** Library of Congress LC-DIG-ppmsca-40789. **Page 61:** Courtesy National Archives photo no. 111-SC-008716. **Page 63:** Library of Congress LC-DIG-stereo-1s04193. **Page 64:** Library of Congress LC-DIG-stereo-1s04178. **Page 66:** Library of Congress LC-DIG-ggbain-26979. **Page 68:** Library of Congress LC-DIG-ggbain-26138. **Page 70:** Library of Congress LC-USZC4-1660. **Page 74:** Library of Congress LC-USZ62-55083. **Page 77:** Courtesy National Archives photo no. 165-WW-172(1). **Page 80:** Courtesy National Archives photo no. 165-WW-578B(6). **Page 85:** Library of Congress LC-DIG-npcc-12745. **Page 89:** Courtesy of the National Archives at Kansas City (ARC ID no.2641493). **Page 90:** Courtesy National Archives. **Page 95:** National Archives photo no. 165-WW-39B(3). **Page 96:** Library of Congress LC-DIG-ppmsca-18640. **Page 99:** Library of Congress LC-DIG-ppmsca-11464. **Page 100:** Horace Pippin memoir of his experiences in World War I, ca. 1921. Horace Pippin notebooks and letters, circa 1920, 1943. Archives of American Art, Smithsonian Institution. **Page 103:** Library of Congress LC-USZ62-116442. **Page 106:** Library of Congress LC-USZ62-46395. **Page 108:** Courtesy National Archives photo no. 165-WW-127(12). **Page 111:** Courtesy National Archives photo no. 165-WW-127-24. **Page 112:** Library of Congress LC-USZC4-9863. **Page 115:** Library of Congress LC-DIG-npcc-32664. **Page 117:** Courtesy National Archives photo no. 111- SC-31731. **Page 118:** National Archives photo no. War and Conflict 436. **Page 121:** Library of Congress LC-DIG-ds-03989. **Pages 122–23:** Courtesy National Archives photo no. 165-WW-581A-1. **Page 126:** Library of Congress LC-USZC4-10654. **Page 129:** Library of Congress LC-DIG-ggbain-299038. **Page 131:** Library of Congress LC-DIG-stereo-1s04278. **Page 132:** Courtesy *Los Angeles Times*. **Page 136:** Library of Congress LC-USZC4-9884. **Page 138:** Library of Congress LC-DIG-ggbain-31205. **Page 140:** Library of Congress LC-DIG-npcc-22946. **Page 143:** Library of Congress LC-DIG-ppmsca-09634. **Page 145:** Library of Congress HABS DC-857-7. **Page 146:** Library of Congress LC-USZC2-6141. **Page 148:** National Archives photo no. 111-SC-23134. **Page 149:** National Archives photo no. 111-SC-16561. **Page 152:** National Archives photo no. 111-SC-18580. **Page 154:** Library of Congress Manuscript ID no. MSS12294.

Acknowledgments

It takes a village to make a book. Mine starts with Howard Reeves, my editor for our fourth book together. His questions, curiosity, enthusiasm, and support have made me a better writer. Thanks, too, to Pamela Notarantonio for her striking design, which brings alive the images and the text. Editorial assistant Masha Gunic deftly handled the continual flow of drafts, emails, and the rare bit of snail mail. Orlando Dos Reis, assistant editor, made excellent suggestions to enliven the book.

I am grateful to managing editor James Armstrong, who dealt with what sometimes seemed like endless editorial changes with speed and grace. Copyeditor Renée Cafiero and fact-checker David M. Webster are expert at improving accuracy and nuance. I appreciate the production work of Kathy Lovisolo and the marketing skill of Jason Wells and Nicole Russo, as well as the efforts of the sales team and all the other folks at Abrams.

Many thanks to Peggy Wagner, who was writing a book on the United States in World War I for adults. Our conversations and her thoughtful insights inspired me to write this one for children. Ray Skean and I have been exchanging books and encouraging each other's interest in World War I for years. His remarkable collection of primary sources and memorabilia were invaluable in developing my ideas.

I am also grateful to Athena Angelos for sharing the wealth of World War I images she had researched and making it possible for me to include them. Friends and Library of Congress colleagues Susan Reyburn, Aimee Hess Nash, and Peter Devereaux also helped with images and have been a cheering section for my work for years.

Special thanks to my husband, Bob; my daughter, Catherine; and my daughter-in-law, Mary Kate Hurley. They spend endless hours willingly listening to every story and fact I have to tell. And, as always, thanks to my son, Nick, a professor of American history, for guiding me, reading and carefully editing my manuscript, and understanding how exciting it is to love and learn about history.

Index

Note: Page numbers in *italics* refer to illustrations.

African Americans, *96*, 97–111, *103*, *108*, *111*
  discrimination against, 98, 100-101, 105, 107, 108-9, 124
  jobs for, 105–9, *106*
  lynchings, 107–8
  race riots, 107, 109, 139
  women, *106*, 119, 125
airplanes, *66*, 67–68, 73
Allied Countries, 1, 137, 141
American Civil Liberties Union, 93
American Expeditionary Force (AEF), 40, 43
American Federation of Labor (AFL), 90–91
American Medical Corps, *47*
armistice, 52, *53*, *143*
artillery, 55, 56, 62, *148*
Austro-Hungarian Empire, 1, 7–9, 12–14, 17, 49
Belgium, U.S. aid to, *154*
Berger, Victor, *85*, 87
Big Four, *129*, 130
Bolshevik Revolution (1917), 17, 50, 141
bombs, *5*, *138*
Boy Scouts, *95*
Britain:
  blockade of Germany, *22*, 23–24, 26, 32
  empire of, 12, 16–17
  treaties with, 13, 14
  and war's end, 130

Browning automatic rifle, 60–61
Bush, George W., 142
cavalry, 55, 56, *57*
censorship, 84–86, 88, 94, 141
Central Powers, 1
civil disobedience, 114–16, *115*
Clemenceau, Georges, *129*
Committee on Public Information (CPI), 82–84, 87–88
communism, 139–41
conscientious objectors (COs), 38–39, 93–94
Creel, George, 82
Debs, Eugene, *85*, 86–87
democracy, 4, 31, 35, 71, 116
Depression, 142
doughboys, *39*, 40, *99*
draft boards, 38–40, 98, 101
Du Bois, W. E. B., 98, 110
electricity, restrictions on, 76
Espionage Act, 84, 85, 86–87, 88, 116
Europe, map, *10–11*
FBI (Federal Bureau of Investigation), 140–41
field guns, 57, *59*
flamethrowers, 51, 62
flu epidemic, 51, 121, 123
Food Administration, 78
Four Minute Men, 82–83
Fourteen Points, 128–29, 133, 141
France:
  African Americans in, 109–10

Croix de Guerre award, 105, 111
empire of, 12, 16–17
fighting in, 46–49, *49*, 50–52, 104
treaties with, 13, 14
U.S. Army in, 38, *41*, *121*
and war's end, 130
Franz Ferdinand, 7–8, *9*, 14, 18
Fuel Administration, 78
gas, as weapon, 62–65
gas masks, *63*, 64–65
Germany:
 British blockade of, 22, 23–24, 26, 32
 empire of, 9, 12, 17
 and Mexico, 33
 prejudice against, 92
 ships torpedoed by, 2, *3*, 25–26, *25*,
  32, 33
 war declared on, 1–2, 14, 37
 and war's end, 128–33, 141
government bureaucracy, 94, 141
Great Migration, 107, 119
grenades, 61–62
Hague Conventions, 24
home front, 71–95
Hoover, Herbert, 78, *140*
"Human Squirrel," *80*
immigrants, 1, 24, 26–27, 30, 87–89,
  89, 90, 92, 105, 140
India, soldiers from, *16*
Industrial Workers of the World
 (IWW), *90*, 91–92
isolationism, 138–39
Italy:
 fighting in, 48–49
 and war's end, 130
Japan, 14
jobs, 72–73, *74*, 105–9, *106*, *117*

Johnson, Henry, 104–5
"Lafayette Escadrille," 27
League of Nations, 132, 134–35
Liberty bonds, 78–79, 88, 125, *149*
Lloyd George, David, *129*
Lost Battalion, 52
Lusitania, 25–26, 28, 33, 71
lynching, 91–92, 107–8
machine guns, 60, *61*
Mexican Revolution, 28–29
Mexico, and Germany, 33
National Defense Act, 29
Nineteenth Amendment, 116
Obama, Barack, 144
100 percent American, 87–88, 94
Orlando, Vittorio, *129*
pacifists, 1, 29–30, 39, 72
Pancho Villa, 28–29
patriotism, 34, 114, 117, 119, 124
peace, 127–35
peace movement, 29–31, *30*, 71, 113
Pershing, General John J., 29, 43, 103,
  105
Pippin, Horace, *100*, 101–3
preparedness, 1, 21, 27–29, *28*, 37, 38,
  72–73
Princip, Gavrilo, 7, 8
Progressive Movement, 30–31, 71, 87
propaganda, 81–84, 94
Railroad Administration, 78
rationing, 73–75
Red Cross, *95*, 120–23, *121*
Richtofen, Manfred von ("Red Baron"),
  67
Rickenbacker, Eddie, 67
Roosevelt, Theodore, 27, 31, 138
Russia, 12, 13, 14, 17–18, 50

Sedition Act, 85, 86–87

segregation, 98, 100–101, 105, 107, 108–9, 124

Selective Service Act, 38

shells, 57–58, 148

shell shock, 58–60

socialists, 31, 86–88, 91, 109

Soviet Union, 17–18, 141

strikes, 90–91, 107, 139

submarines, 24–25, 68–69, *68*, 71

suffrage (voting rights), 113–16

tanks, *64*, 65–67, *146*

taxes, 78, 79, 81, 94, 142

Treaty of Versailles, 130–34, *131*, 141

trenches, 43–45, *44*, *46*, *48*, 56–57, 58, 62

U-boats, 24–25, 68–69, *68*, 71

unions, 88, 90–91

United States:

    armed forces, 37–42

    entry into war, 1–2, 17, 33–35, 49

    isolationism of, 138–39, 142

    jobs in, 72–73

    neutrality of, 1, 21–34, 138

    war at home, 71–95

    war economy of, 72, 137, *140*

    in world trade, 2, 22–24, 34, 72, 139, 141–42

U.S. Army, 40, 98, 101–5, *103*, *108*

    women's work in, 120–24, *121*, *122–23*

U.S. Navy, *40*, 41–42

    women's reserve forces, *118*, 120

victory gardens, 75–76, *77*, 125

voting rights, 113–16, 125

War Industries Board, 78

weapons, 55–69

welfare workers, 124

White, Bertha Hale, *85*

Wilhelm II, Kaiser, 2, *33*, 130

Wilson, Woodrow:

    Fourteen Points, 128–29, 133, 141

    and Germany, 2, 4, 32, 71

    ideals of, 71, 142, 144

    and League of Nations, *132*, 134–35

    and peace, 2, 31, 37, 71, 138

    and preparedness, 29, 37, 38, 72

    and war declaration, 1, 2

    and war's end, 127–30, *129*, 131, 139

women, 113–25

    African American, *106*, 119

    farming, *122–23*

    jobs for, *74*, *106*, 117–20, *117*

    lower pay for, 119, 125

    in military, *118*, 120–24

    nurses, 120–21, *121*

    traditional roles of, 124–25

    voting rights for, 113–16, 125

workers' rights, 88, 90

World War I:

    deaths in, 2, 4, 49

    effects of, 4, 133, 137–44

    end of, 2, 52, *53*, 127–35, *143*

    memorials, *145*

    nations drawn into, 14, 33

    profits from, 31, 34, 72–73

    as total war, 72, 94

    truce in, 2

World War II, 133

Zimmermann Telegram, 33